STANDARDS OF PRACTICE CASEBOOK

©1996, Association for Investment Management and Research

This publication is designed to provide accurate and authoritative information in regard to the subject matter covered. It is sold with the understanding that the publisher is not engaged in rendering legal, accounting, or other professional service. If legal advice or other expert assistance is required, the services of a competent professional should be sought.

ISBN 1-879087-76-6

Printed in the United States of America

September 1996

Contents

Foreword

AIMR is dedicated to serving its members and, through them, serving investors as a global leader in education, in examining investment managers' and analysts' skills and knowledge, and in sustaining high standards of professional conduct. To accomplish its mission, AIMR members continuously work to maintain high standards of education and ethics for its members, Chartered Financial Analyst charterholders, and CFA® candidates. This casebook is the latest of many resources developed to educate and enlighten investment professionals about the fundamental aspects of their professional practice and responsibilities.

The *Standards of Practice Casebook* was designed primarily as a learning tool for candidates in the CFA Program. The book will assist all CFA charterholders and AIMR members, however, to understand their obligations under AIMR's Code of Ethics, Standards of Professional Conduct, and where applicable, Performance Presentation Standards (PPS). These elements of AIMR's Professional Conduct Program are critical ingredients in AIMR's efforts to promote professionalism in the investment industry. AIMR's intention in putting together this casebook is to provide discussion of and practice in applying the Code, the Standards, and the PPS. The cases can pull together—in a meaningful and easily understood way—the principles and tenets of professional practice in investment management.

We appreciate the valuable contributions of numerous people who provided insights and practical material for this casebook. For the cases themselves, we wish to thank Glen A. Holden, Jr., CFA, The Capitol Life Insurance Company; Douglas R. Hughes, CFA; Jules Huot, CFA, Pension Commission of Ontario; Amy F. Lipton, CFA, Bankers Trust; Scott L. Lummer, CFA, Ibbotson Associates; Paul F. Van Schyndel, CFA, State Street Global Advisors; and Gordon T. Wise, CFA, Gordon T. Wise and Company. We also wish to thank Sam Jones, chair of the Standards of Practice Subcommittee of the PCP and ethics coordinator for the 1995–96 Council of Examiners; W. Scott Bauman, CFA; Lucinda Hastings, CFA; William Koenig, CFA; Barbara Palk, CFA; and Joanne L. Yachimec for their thoughtful comments on the cases.

We hope that you find this product useful in expanding your ability to understand and apply AIMR's approach to professional responsibilities. Because this casebook is the first we have attempted on the Professional Conduct Program, we look forward even more than usual to your response to the *Standards of Practice Casebook*. Please send us your reactions, comments, and suggestions.

Michael S. Caccese, Esq.   Katrina F. Sherrerd, CFA
Senior Vice President,   Senior Vice President
General Counsel,   Educational Products
Secretary

Introduction

The *Standards of Practice Casebook* is designed to assist the reader in identifying violations of the AIMR Code of Ethics, Standards of Professional Conduct, and Performance Presentation Standards (AIMR PPS) and in understanding the appropriate response to ethically challenging situations. The *Casebook* contains fictional (but realistic) cases and briefs of actual regulatory violations. The cases are designed to present issues in a way that closely approximates how individuals practicing in the investment industry encounter ethical issues in their day-to-day activities. The discussions following each case identify the violations of the Standards and recommend corrective actions. The discussions also provide guidance for establishing relevant organizational policy statements and adequate compliance procedures. The case briefs provide short summaries of actual legal and professional conduct violations and the sanctions imposed.

How to Use the *Casebook*

The *Casebook* is designed to expand the reader's basic knowledge of the Code, Standards, and AIMR PPS gained from both the *Standards of Practice Handbook* (1996 edition) and the *Performance Presentation Standards*. By presenting real and real-world but hypothetical situations containing one or more instances of unethical behavior or professional misconduct, the *Casebook* aims to promote understanding of how potentially unethical and unprofessional situations can develop; the discussions add the perspective of the Code and Standards to situations in which the ethical dimensions may not be entirely clear. The goal is not only to promote understanding of the Code, Standards, and AIMR PPS but also to show how to apply them in the real world. For ease of reference, we have included the Code and simple statements of the Standards at the opening of the book; readers should turn to the *Handbook* and *Performance Presentation Standards*, however, for full discussions of standards.

Each case challenges the reader to identify the *key* violations illustrated in the case. Although all violations are equally significant, the case discussions focus on the major violations in order to emphasize the importance of those issues and to simplify the discussion. In combination, the cases provide coverage of all key elements of AIMR's Code, Standards, and PPS. In most of the cases, in addition to the key violations discussed, one or more of the following also apply, and the actors in the cases would have to comply with these principles:

- **Code of Ethics**. In every situation, AIMR members, CFA charterholders, and candidates in the CFA Program have a duty to conduct themselves with integrity and dignity and to act in an ethical manner. Members, charterholders, and candidates must act with competence, use proper care, and exercise independent judgment in their professional practices.

- **Standard I, Fundamental Responsibilities**. AIMR members, CFA charterholders, and CFA candidates must maintain knowledge of and must comply with all applicable laws, rules, and regulations of any government, governmental agency, regulatory organization, licensing agency, or professional association governing the members' professional activities. Members, charterholders, and candidates must not knowingly participate in or assist any violation of such laws, rules, or regulations. They should ensure that they have appropriate knowledge of the laws and regulations of all countries in which they practice.

- **Standard II(B), Professional Misconduct**. AIMR members, CFA charterholders, and CFA candidates must not engage in any professional conduct involving dishonesty, fraud, deceit, or misrepresentation and must not commit any act that reflects adversely on their honesty, trustworthiness, or professional competence.

- **Standard III(A), Duty to Inform Employer of Code and Standards**. AIMR members, CFA charterholders, and CFA candidates must inform their employer, through their direct supervisor, that they are obligated to comply with the Code and Standards and are subject to disciplinary sanctions for violating this obligation. Members, charterholders, and candidates must deliver a copy of the Code and Standards to their employer if the employer does not have a copy.

- **Standard III(E), Responsibilities of Supervisors**. AIMR members, CFA charterholders, and CFA candidates with supervisory responsibility, authority, or the ability to influence the conduct of others must exercise reasonable supervision over those subject to their supervision or authority in order to prevent any violation of applicable statutes, regulations, or provisions of the Code and Standards. Supervisors must exercise their supervisory responsibility with *all* employees under their control, even those employees who are not AIMR members, CFA charterholders, or CFA candidates.

AIMR's Disciplinary Process

The case briefs present short synopses of actual instances of professional misconduct and the related regulatory sanctions that were imposed. Although the individuals in the case briefs were sanctioned only by regulatory bodies, had they been members of AIMR, CFA charterholders, or CFA candidates, their conduct would have subjected them to the disciplinary process of AIMR's Professional Conduct Program (PCP). Similarly, if a member, charterholder, or candidate were to violate the Code or Standards in ways described in the case briefs, AIMR's PCP would have the authority to punish them.

The enforcement effort of the PCP is based on three principles:

- fair process to the member, charterholder, or candidate,
- confidentiality of proceedings, and
- peer review.

The AIMR Board of Governors maintains oversight and responsibility for the PCP, but professional conduct investigations are conducted by AIMR's PCP staff under the supervision of AIMR's Designated Officer and the Professional Standards and Policy Committee. Anyone can write the PCP with a complaint regarding the professional conduct of any member or candidate, and the PCP will initiate an inquiry into the member's conduct to determine if a violation of the Code or Standards has occurred. If the Designated Officer determines that disciplinary action is appropriate, the matter is turned over to a review panel drawn from AIMR members involved with the PCP. These panels conduct a hearing on the matter or, if the member has entered into a stipulation with the Designated Officer agreeing to a sanction, review the stipulated agreement.

AIMR members, CFA charterholders, and CFA candidates who violate the Code and Standards will be sanctioned. Authorized sanctions include— in increasing order of severity—private censure, public censure, suspension of membership, revocation of membership, and in the case of CFA charterholders, suspension and revocation of the CFA designation. CFA candidates found to be violating the Code and Standards may be suspended from further participation in the CFA Program.

The Code of Ethics

Members of the Association for Investment Management and Research shall:

- Act with integrity, competence, dignity, and in an ethical manner when dealing with the public, clients, prospects, employers, employees, and fellow members.
- Practice and encourage others to practice in a professional and ethical manner that will reflect credit on members and their profession.
- Strive to maintain and improve their competence and the competence of others in the profession.
- Use reasonable care and exercise independent professional judgment.

Statement of

The Standards of Professional Conduct

Standard I: Fundamental Responsibilities

Members shall:

A.   Maintain knowledge of and comply with all applicable laws, rules, and regulations (including AIMR's Code of Ethics and Standards of Professional Conduct) of any government, governmental agency, regulatory organization, licensing agency, or professional association governing the members' professional activities.

B.   Not knowingly participate or assist in any violation of such laws, rules, or regulations.

Standard II: Relationships with and Responsibilities to the Profession

A.   **Use of Professional Designation.**

1.   Membership in AIMR, the Financial Analyst Federation (FAF), or the Institute of Chartered Financial Analysts (ICFA) may be referenced by members of these organizations only in a dignified and judicious manner. The use of the reference may be accompanied by an accurate explanation of the requirements that have been met to obtain membership in these organizations.

2.   Holders of the Chartered Financial Analyst designation may use the professional designation "Chartered Financial Analyst," or the mark "CFA," and are encouraged to do so, but only in a dignified and judicious manner. The use of the designation may be accompanied by an accurate explanation of the requirements that have been met to obtain the designation.

3.   Candidates may reference their participation in the CFA Program, but the reference must clearly state that an individual is a candidate for the CFA designation and may not imply that the candidate has achieved any type of partial designation.

B.   **Professional Misconduct.** Members shall not engage in any professional conduct involving dishonesty, fraud, deceit, or misrepresentation or commit any act that reflects adversely on their honesty, trustworthiness, or professional competence.

C.   **Prohibition against Plagiarism.** Members shall not copy or use, in substantially the same form as the original, material prepared by another without acknowledging and identifying the name of the author, publisher, or source of such material. Members may use, without acknowledgment, factual information published by recognized financial and statistical reporting services or similar sources.

Standard III: Relationships with and Responsibilities to the Employer

A.   **Obligation to Inform Employer of Code and Standards.** Members shall:

   1.   Inform their employer, through their direct supervisor, that they are obligated to comply with the Code and Standards and are subject to disciplinary sanctions for violations thereof.

   2.   Deliver a copy of the Code and Standards to their employer if the employer does not have a copy.

B.   **Duty to Employer.** Members shall not undertake any independent practice that could result in compensation or other benefit in competition with their employer unless they obtain written consent from both their employer and the persons or entities for whom they undertake independent practice.

C.   **Disclosure of Conflicts to Employer.** Members shall:

   1.   Disclose to their employer all matters, including beneficial ownership of securities or other investments, that reasonably could be expected to interfere with their duty to their employer or ability to make unbiased and objective recommendations.

   2.   Comply with any prohibitions on activities imposed by their employer if a conflict of interest exists.

D.   **Disclosure of Additional Compensation Arrangements.** Members shall disclose to their employer in writing all monetary compensation or other benefits that they receive for their services that are in addition to compensation or benefits conferred by a member's employer.

E.   **Responsibilities of Supervisors.** Members with supervisory responsibility, authority, or the ability to influence the conduct of others shall exercise reasonable supervision over those subject to their supervision or authority to prevent any violation of applicable statutes, regulations, or provisions of the Code and Standards. In so doing, members are entitled to rely on reasonable procedures designed to detect and prevent such violations.

Standard IV. Relationships with and Responsibilities to Clients and Prospects

A.   **Investment Process.**

A.1   **Reasonable Basis and Representations.** Members shall:

   a.   Exercise diligence and thoroughness in making investment recommendations or in taking investment actions.

   b.   Have a reasonable and adequate basis, supported by appropriate research and investigation, for such recommendations or actions.

c. Make reasonable and diligent efforts to avoid any material misrepresentation in any research report or investment recommendation.

d. Maintain appropriate records to support the reasonableness of such recommendations or actions.

A.2 Research Reports. Members shall:

a. Use reasonable judgment regarding the inclusion or exclusion of relevant factors in research reports.

b. Distinguish between facts and opinions in research reports.

c. Indicate the basic characteristics of the investment involved when preparing for public distribution a research report that is not directly related to a specific portfolio or client.

A.3 Independence and Objectivity. Members shall use reasonable care and judgment to achieve and maintain independence and objectivity in making investment recommendations or taking investment action.

B. Interactions with Clients and Prospects.

B.1 Fiduciary Duties. In relationships with clients, members shall use particular care in determining applicable fiduciary duty and shall comply with such duty as to those persons and interests to whom the duty is owed. Members must act for the benefit of their clients and place their clients' interests before their own.

B.2 Portfolio Investment Recommendations and Actions. Members shall:

a. Make a reasonable inquiry into a client's financial situation, investment experience, and investment objectives prior to making any investment recommendations and shall update this information as necessary, but no less frequently than annually, to allow the members to adjust their investment recommendations to reflect changed circumstances.

b. Consider the appropriateness and suitability of investment recommendations or actions for each portfolio or client. In determining appropriateness and suitability, members shall consider applicable relevant factors, including the needs and circumstances of the portfolio or client, the basic characteristics of the investment involved, and the basic characteristics of the total portfolio. Members shall not make a recommendation unless they reasonably determine that the recommendation is suitable to the client's financial situation, investment experience, and investment objectives.

c. Distinguish between facts and opinions in the presentation of investment recommendations.

    d.   Disclose to clients and prospects the basic format and general principles of the investment processes by which securities are selected and portfolios are constructed and shall promptly disclose to clients and prospects any changes that might significantly affect those processes.

B.3 Fair Dealing. Members shall deal fairly and objectively with all clients and prospects when disseminating investment recommendations, disseminating material changes in prior investment recommendations, and taking investment action.

B.4 Priority of Transactions. Transactions for clients and employers shall have priority over transactions in securities or other investments of which a member is the beneficial owner so that such personal transactions do not operate adversely to their clients' or employer's interests. If members make a recommendation regarding the purchase or sale of a security or other investment, they shall give their clients and employer adequate opportunity to act on the recommendation before acting on their own behalf. For purposes of the Code and Standards, a member is a "beneficial owner" if the member has

    a.   a direct or indirect pecuniary interest in the securities;

    b.   the power to vote or direct the voting of the shares of the securities or investments;

    c.   the power to dispose or direct the disposition of the security or investment.

B.5 Preservation of Confidentiality. Members shall preserve the confidentiality of information communicated by clients, prospects, or employers concerning matters within the scope of the client–member, prospect–member, or employer–member relationship unless the member receives information concerning illegal activities on the part of the client, prospect, or employer.

B.6 Prohibition against Misrepresentation. Members shall not make any statements, orally or in writing, that misrepresent

    a.   the services that they or their firms are capable of performing;

    b.   their qualifications or the qualifications of their firm;

    c.   the member's academic or professional credentials.

Members shall not make or imply, orally or in writing, any assurances or guarantees regarding any investment except to communicate accurate information regarding the terms of the investment instrument and the issuer's obligations under the instrument.

B.7 Disclosure of Conflicts to Clients and Prospects. Members shall disclose to their clients and prospects all matters, including beneficial ownership of securities or other investments, that reasonably could be expected to impair the member's ability to make unbiased and objective recommendations.

B.8 Disclosure of Referral Fees. Members shall disclose to clients and prospects any consideration or benefit received by the member or delivered to others for the recommendation of any services to the client or prospect.

Standard V. Relationships with and Responsibilities to the Investing Public

A. Prohibition against Use of Material Nonpublic Information. Members who possess material nonpublic information related to the value of a security shall not trade or cause others to trade in that security if such trading would breach a duty or if the information was misappropriated or relates to a tender offer. If members receive material nonpublic information in confidence, they shall not breach that confidence by trading or causing others to trade in securities to which such information relates. Members shall make reasonable efforts to achieve public dissemination of material nonpublic information disclosed in breach of a duty.

B. Performance Presentation.

1. Members shall not make any statements, orally or in writing, that misrepresent the investment performance that they or their firms have accomplished or can reasonably be expected to achieve.

2. If members communicate individual or firm performance information directly or indirectly to clients or prospective clients, or in a manner intended to be received by clients or prospective clients, members shall make every reasonable effort to assure that such performance information is a fair, accurate, and complete presentation of such performance.

The Snake Fund

Case Facts

Jake Dose is thrilled to receive the letter from AIMR stating that he has successfully completed Level III of the CFA exam, met all the other requirements, and is now a charterholder. Dose's career has progressed well since he joined his father at Dose & Son Advisory (D&S) five years ago, and he believes that earning the CFA designation is a major milestone in his life. How proud his father would have been! Three weeks earlier, his father suffered a fatal heart attack. Now, as the sole heir to the business, Dose is contemplating how he will go forward.

D&S is a small, successful investment advisory business registered with the U.S. Securities and Exchange Commission. The firm has a broad-based clientele made up of private accounts and small businesses' pension and profit-sharing plans and has 90 clients in equity accounts worth approximately $100 million. D&S has a conservative investment style, with returns closely matching the S&P 500 Index.

Until his father's death, Jake Dose's responsibilities were in the analysis of individual securities, and he was not involved in day-to-day operations or portfolio management at D&S. He had expected to become more involved in such areas, however, because his father had considered the achievement of the CFA designation to be a stepping stone for his son to take on more responsibility at the firm.

As the new president of D&S, Dose wonders what effect the news of his father's death will have on D&S's clients. He wants to keep the firm in business, and he believes he would never make as much money working for another investment firm. Dose is afraid that if he tells clients outright about his father's death and his own lack of portfolio management experience, they will leave. Perhaps hiring an experienced individual to replace his father would be the best decision, but a new person might one day walk out the door with all of D&S's clients.

In order to retain the firm's clients, Dose decides to gloss over the fact that he has not actually managed money. He convinces the clients that he has worked side by side with his father on all matters concerning their portfolios. He also tells clients that, as a CFA charterholder, he is certified to perform all aspects of money management. Dose is so persuasive that he convinces most clients to stay with the firm.

Dose is not fooling himself, however; he knows how to go about

This case was written by Paul F. Van Schyndel, CFA, State Street Global Advisors.

analyzing individual securities, but he is not confident about putting together a portfolio of securities for the D&S clients. He decides that he needs to buy some time to get organized and figure out what to do with each client's account. He is also worried that stock market valuations are unrealistically high at this time. So, he moves all of his clients' funds out of individual securities and into a money market mutual fund.

In the next few months, while Dose is figuring out his investment strategy, the stock market moves steadily higher. Clients begin to call Dose and ask him why they are earning only 3 percent annualized in their accounts when the stock market has returned 12 percent in only three months. Dose spends many sleepless nights worrying that his clients will desert him unless he takes action to boost their portfolio returns dramatically.

About this time, an old college friend of Dose's, Angus Bilkmore, invites Dose to lunch. Bilkmore is currently managing a limited partnership called the Snake Fund that is invested in emerging market equities in Latin America. During lunch, Bilkmore thrills Dose with stories about his fund producing returns of 30–60 percent since the fund's inception two years ago. Bilkmore also mentions that he is looking for more investors, which would allow him to diversify the investments into other emerging markets around the world.

Dose, thinking that the Snake Fund is the answer to his performance problems, asks about investing his clients' money in the fund. Bilkmore is interested, but he indicates that putting all of D&S's clients into the Snake Fund could be difficult. The Snake Fund, as a limited partnership, is required to keep the number of investors below 100. With more investors, it would become an investment company under the Investment Company Act of 1940 (1940 Act). Both Dose and Bilkmore want to avoid registering any entity as an investment company in order to stay away from the heavy regulatory burden and expenses entailed by registered status, which would include examinations of a firm's operations by SEC staff and independent auditors. So, Dose returns to his office to figure out how to structure a deal with Bilkmore so that neither partnership winds up as an investment company.

After thinking about the issue for several weeks, Dose decides that he will set up his own limited partnership, keeping the number of investors under 100. He will take on the position of general partner, pool all the funds invested in the partnership, and invest the pooled funds in the Snake Fund. He decides to call the limited partnership Ebb & Flow (EF). Because EF is a separate entity, it is considered to be only one investor investing in the Snake Fund. The plan will reduce the chances of Bilkmore's fund becoming an investment company under the 1940 Act, and Bilkmore readily agrees to it.

Dose makes the investments in the EF partnership and the Snake Fund as planned. Thinking that his clients might be confused about this new arrangement, he does not immediately communicate to them that their money market investments have been moved into a portfolio of emerging market securities. He wants to wait until the performance of the Snake Fund begins to affect their portfolios before informing his clients of their investment in EF. Dose mentions the EF investment to his clients but only as part of the broad, general guidelines for investments that might be made by the partnership. Dose does not describe the investments the EF partnership has already made in the Snake Fund or the Snake Fund's emerging market investments.

The Snake Fund turns in a sizzling performance in the next six months, easily outperforming the S&P 500. Dose's clients are naturally pleased with their returns. In fact, they are so happy that they start to flood D&S with additional funds to invest in their accounts. Friends and relatives of D&S clients also start to send investable funds to Dose.

As the number of partners in the EF partnership quickly approaches the 1940 Act limit, Dose decides to set up a new partnership to handle this investor demand. He calls it Ebb & Flow II (EFII), and rather than investing directly into the Snake Fund, Dose decides to invest EFII's assets into EF first and then, through EF, invest it in the Snake Fund. In this way, Dose can contain the number of entities investing in the Snake Fund and help Bilkmore keep his fund from becoming an investment company.

Dose, as the general partner of EF and EFII, receives a fee for managing the partnerships. As the investment advisor to the limited partners in the EF and EFII partnerships, he also receives advisory fees. Dose wonders whether he should find a way to reduce or eliminate some of the fees clients are paying, particularly for the EFII partnership, or tell clients about the fee arrangements. The handsome returns being generated by the Snake Fund, however, convince Dose that he is adding to his clients' wealth substantially, so he believes the fees are justified.

To occupy his time, Dose researches securities that he or Bilkmore identify as potential candidates for inclusion in the Snake Fund. Because of his expertise in securities analysis, Dose believes that if the stock picks he gives Bilkmore are good and are added to the Snake Fund, he can help his friend and boost the returns on his clients' investments.

For two years, the Snake Fund does very well, with returns well over 35 percent in one year and 55 percent the next. In the following two years, however, things begin to sour. The Snake Fund has a zero return in one year and a negative return the year after that. In these two years of flat or negative performance by the Snake Fund, the S&P 500 reaches record highs every quarter. Again, clients begin to call Dose and question the difference between their returns and those of the S&P 500.

Dose thinks he should look for alternative investments for his clients, so he gets together over lunch with Bilkmore to discuss the matter. Bilkmore tells Dose that now is a bad time to get out of the Snake Fund and that valuations are so low they must surely go up soon. Bilkmore also indicates that liquidity in most emerging markets has dried up and that only the securities of the best-known, large-capitalization companies can be traded easily. In addition, Dose's partnership accounts for the largest investment in the Snake Fund, and the removal of such a large amount of money would have a major negative effect on the fund. Bilkmore also tells Dose that he is so impressed with Dose's stock selections he has decided to pay Dose for his ideas. Every quarter, Bilkmore will send Dose a $75,000 check for his investment recommendations.

After lunch, Dose decides to postpone moving money out of the Snake Fund in the hope that emerging markets will turn up soon. He makes one exception, however, for his Uncle Ed, one of the largest clients at D&S, who has been asking Dose for his money so he can invest it elsewhere at higher returns. Because his uncle was one of the first investors at D&S when his father started the business and helped get D&S up and running and because of the family connection, Dose believes he must honor this request. For the moment, he dissuades other clients who have been making the same request from removing their money. Dose believes he is a good securities analyst and thinks that if he can provide Bilkmore with some very successful investment ideas, the performance of the Snake Fund will rebound.

In the next year, Dose does in fact give Bilkmore several investment ideas, but only two prove useful. Dose begins to wonder if he is worth what Bilkmore is paying him. Could his friend be paying him simply to keep Dose's clients in the Snake Fund? Because he is a little uncomfortable about the financial arrangement, he does not tell anyone about it, including his clients. Nevertheless, he cashes the quarterly checks from Bilkmore.

> *Identify the activities at D&S that are or could be in violation of the AIMR Code of Ethics and Standards of Professional Conduct. State what actions Dose could have taken or could take now to eliminate the potential violations. Make a short policy statement a firm could use to prevent the violations.*

Case Discussion

The potential violations evident in this case relate to Jake Dose's many illegal activities, his misrepresentation of his firm's investment services, his lack of fair dealing with clients, and his breach of fiduciary duty to clients. Dose also failed to use the CFA designation in an appropriate manner.

Compliance with Governing Laws and Regulations. Dose broke the law in two areas: operating an unregistered investment company and failing to provide clients with full and fair disclosure of all fee arrangements.

■ *An unregistered investment company.* By layering the Ebb & Flow and Ebb & Flow II limited partnerships, both of which have virtually identical investment objectives and which, combined, have more than the 100-investor limit allowed by law, Dose formed an unregistered investment company and is in violation of the 1940 Act and SEC rules and regulations regarding the registration of an investment company with more than 100 investors. Dose also violated Standard I, Fundamental Responsibilities, which requires him to know and comply with all laws, rules, and regulations governing his professional, financial, and business activities.

Actions required. Dose cannot do indirectly that which would be illegal to do directly, so he should not have set up layered partnerships to skirt the law. Dose should have familiarized himself with all rules and regulations applicable to his business and verified that he was complying with those laws. If he was uncertain about applying the law to his business, then he should have sought the advice of competent legal counsel.

> *Policy statement for a firm.* "The firm shall take reasonable and adequate steps to ensure that it is in compliance with the law and with all rules and regulations applicable to its business. At a minimum, an annual review of the firm's business activities shall be conducted to determine if any changes have occurred in the firm's business practices or in regulatory requirements. If any changes are needed as a result of such review, they shall be implemented immediately."

■ *Full and fair disclosure of fee arrangements.* The 1940 Act requires full and fair disclosure of fee arrangements to clients. Dose had an obligation to disclose his fee arrangements fully to his clients, particularly his charging equity management fees for the management of money market accounts and his double billing of fees by charging for EF and EFII. Investment advisory fees should be commensurate with the services provided. Charging unreasonable fees violates Standard IV(B.3), Fair Dealing.

Overbilling in this situation was not only illegal but also unethical. It violated the first tenet for the investment professional in AIMR's Code, which requires members to "act with integrity, competence, dignity, and in an ethical manner when dealing with the public, clients, prospects, employers, employees, and fellow [AIMR] members."

Actions required. At all times, Dose should have provided full and fair disclosure to his clients of all fee arrangements and, prior to billing clients for such services, should have disclosed his billing practices. Dose should immediately rebate double-billed fees to clients.

> *Policy statement for a firm.* "Fees charged shall be commensurate with the services provided. Accounts shall be periodically reviewed to determine if fees being charged are proper. If a review of accounts reveals that some have been double billed, the fees shall be rebated. If fees are found to be excessive, they shall be reduced to an appropriate level."

Portfolio Investment Recommendations and Actions.

The violations that resulted from Dose's investment actions include a failure to inform his clients of material changes in the management style for their portfolios and a failure to consider the appropriateness of his investment actions for clients.

■ *Disclosure of changes in the firm's investment process.* Dose violated Standard IV(B.2), Portfolio Investment Recommendations and Actions, when he failed to disclose promptly to his clients the change in management from fully invested equity accounts to a money market mutual fund. His clients expected and were paying for equity money management. He again violated this standard when he neglected to disclose the movement of the clients' assets from the money market fund to EF and EFII, a significant change in asset class, style, and investment process.

■ *Appropriateness and suitability of investment actions.* The case states that D&S had "a conservative investment style, with returns closely matching the S&P 500 Index." In placing the firm's clients in the Snake Fund via the limited partnerships, Dose thus violated Standard IV(B.2). Dose did not consider the appropriateness or suitability of emerging market investments for clients accustomed to a conservative approach and did not take into account the clients' needs, circumstances, and objectives before taking investment action. Dose made the investments that would bail him out of trouble with his clients and was lucky, at least for a while, that they did.

Actions required. Before making material changes in his investment process, Dose should have informed his clients of such changes and ensured that they understood and concurred with the changes. Prior to taking investment action for his clients, Dose should have determined that such action was appropriate and suitable for his clients' needs.

> *Policy statement for a firm.* "Prior to making material changes to the firm's investment process, we will fully inform clients of such changes. Any clients who are affected by such changes must agree to them

before we implement the changes. In order to verify suitability, we will also review clients' investment objectives, preferences, and constraints prior to taking investment action."

Misrepresentation of Services. When Dose did not disclose the fact that he had not previously managed money but, in fact, had only analyzed individual securities, he was misrepresenting the services he could perform for clients. By this misrepresentation, Dose violated Standard IV(B.6), Prohibition against Misrepresentation.

Actions required. Dose should have provided only truthful and accurate descriptions of his business experience to clients so that they could make a reasoned judgment about his abilities to manage their money.

> *Policy statement for a firm.* "Clients and prospective clients shall be provided full and fair disclosure of all applicable business experience and education of employees and the services that the firm can provide."

Fair Dealing with Clients. Cashing out Uncle Ed and leaving other clients in a poorly performing investment was not fair to the remaining clients. When the fund sold its most liquid securities to meet Uncle Ed's redemption request, the shareholders left in the fund suffered because of the lack of liquidity of the remaining securities. In favoring his uncle to the detriment of all other clients, Dose violated Standard IV(B.3), Fair Dealing. Dose should not have acted on his uncle's request while ignoring all other clients with similar requests.

Actions required. Dose should have handled all redemption requests in a consistent manner. He should have reviewed the procedures set forth in the partnership agreement regarding the repurchase of partnership units and made sure that those procedures were followed.

> *Policy statement for a firm.* "We will treat all clients in a fair and equitable manner. No client will be favored over another or in such a manner as to harm another client. Repurchase of partnership units shall be handled as set forth in the offering memo."

Disclosure of Potential Conflicts of Interest. The $75,000 quarterly payments Angus Bilkmore made to Dose, supposedly for investment advice, interfered with Dose's ability to render unbiased and objective advice to his clients. Without those payments, Dose might have moved his clients out of the Snake Fund and into more appropriate investments. By not disclosing the financial arrangement and relationship with Bilkmore to his clients, Dose violated Standard IV(B.7), Disclosure of Conflicts to Clients and Prospects.

Actions required. Dose should disclose his additional compensation to all clients and explain that this compensation could cause a conflict of interest between his own and his clients' interests.

> *Policy statement for a firm.* "An employee shall disclose to the firm and to clients any compensation or other benefits received from a person or entity other than the firm for services rendered by the employee that could pose a potential conflict of interest. Additional compensation to employees that would result in a conflict of interest for the employee or the firm is prohibited."

Fiduciary Duties. By failing to act solely in his clients' interests, Dose violated Standard IV(B.1), Fiduciary Duties, in two ways. First, he acted in his own interest instead of his clients' by lying about his experience in order to persuade clients to stay at D&S. Second, he breached his fiduciary duty by keeping his clients' assets in the Snake Fund in return for the $75,000 quarterly checks from Bilkmore. Without D&S's assets, Bilkmore's Snake Fund would have shrunk and Dose's management fees would have been correspondingly reduced as Bilkmore's incentive and ability to pay Dose diminished.

Actions required. Dose should have acted in his clients' best interests and placed their funds in investments that best suited their, not his own, needs. Dose should have disclosed his additional compensation to all clients and should have explained that this compensation could cause a conflict of interest between his own and their interests.

> *Policy statement for a firm.* "At all times, employees shall consider their actions in the context of clients' interests and shall place clients' interests ahead of their own."

Use of Professional Designation. Dose told his clients that he was certified to perform all aspects of money management because he had a CFA charter, which violated Standard II(A), Use of Professional Designation. To imply that simply holding a CFA charter makes an individual able to carry out all aspects of money management is misleading. Such statements do not represent use of the designation in a dignified and judicious manner, and they exceed the permissible explanation of the meaning of the charter specified in the Standards.

Actions required. Dose should have claimed expertise only in the areas in which he actually had expertise and should not have claimed to have any skills that he did not possess. Dose may inform clients that he is a CFA charterholder, but he should also provide an explanation of the requirements involved in achieving the designation so that clients are aware that the designation does not endow anyone with special investment powers.

> ***Policy statement for a firm.*** "Disclosure to clients and prospects of educational and professional designations shall be accompanied by a brief explanation of the requirements and experience involved in achieving such designations."

Showcase Capital Management

Case Facts

Harvey Reynolds, a CFA charterholder, is sitting at his desk in February 1993 looking at the composite performance numbers for his firm, Showcase Capital Management. Although Reynolds obtained the CFA designation before the implementation in January of the AIMR Performance Presentation Standards (PPS), he is confident that he and his partners have followed all the AIMR PPS rules in preparing the presentation of the firm's performance. Reynolds is impressed by the firm's stellar record and is confident that Showcase will land the Stardex account at tomorrow's final presentation.

Harvey Reynolds. In 1984, Reynolds joined the management training group at First National Bank and Trust as an analyst and portfolio manager trainee. In 1989, Reynolds, by then a CFA charterholder, was a vice president and trust officer responsible for a three-person section managing the bank's taxable accounts. He was also a member of his department's investment policy committee, which consisted of three other section heads and the three senior portfolio managers in the department.

The primary equity style of First National at that time was to invest in large-capitalization U.S. companies that demonstrated a consistent ability to increase revenues and earnings. This approach worked well for the bank during the 1980s, and the performance of the bank's Equity Common Trust Fund A for tax-exempt accounts was as follows:

	1983	1984	1985	1986	1987	1988	1989
Common Fund A	24.5%	17.4%	23.7%	18.5%	10.4%	7.3%	28.4%
S&P 500 Index	22.5	6.3	32.2	18.5	5.2	16.8	31.5

One of Reynolds's trust account clients was the widow of Willie Taylor, a long-time employee of the Wal-Mart Stores. Taylor's avid support of the company and affection for Sam Walton caused him to buy Wal-Mart at every opportunity, so that at his death, Taylor had accumulated a sizable position in the company for a man of otherwise modest means. His deathbed admonition to his wife was: "Hang on to that stock and don't

---

This case was written by Gordon T. Wise, CFA, G.T. Wise and Company.

let the bank sell it."

Reynolds had no problem with holding on to the Wal-Mart stock, even though it held a disproportionately large position in the estate, because it had tripled in value in the 1986–89 period. Reynolds developed a close working relationship with Taylor's widow, who relied on him for guidance and counsel following her husband's death.

In mid-1989, Reynolds was approached by Fred Martin, an institutional salesman for a large regional brokerage firm. Martin proposed that the two of them talk to Betty Younger, CFA, a respected portfolio manager at the local City National Bank, about forming a new investment advisory firm. Martin reasoned that if the other two were able to bring some of their clients from the banks, his connections and sales ability would enable the firm to succeed, particularly now that the fear generated by the market crash in October 1987 seemed to be dissipating. Reynolds discussed the proposal with Mrs. Taylor, who was delighted with the prospect of being the first client of a start-up firm. So, Reynolds resigned his position at First National and joined Younger and Martin at the new firm of Showcase Capital Management.

The New Firm. Showcase Capital Management opened its doors on January 1, 1990, with 20 accounts and $15 million under management. Business development was hurt in the first year by the recession and market weakness associated with the Gulf War, but late in the year, Mrs. Taylor added $2 million in cash to her account that she had received upon her brother's death.

During the early years, the partners at Showcase were busy reassuring clients and took little time to attempt to form a definitive investment style. Younger was a strong advocate of the Graham and Dodd value-investing approach, and her portfolios, which experienced below-average performance during this period, focused on companies that she expected to benefit from the resurgence in profitability of "smokestack" America. Reynolds continued to rely on large-cap/growth stocks in his portfolios. Martin, because he did not manage any portfolios, refereed the frequent disputes between Reynolds and Younger about the most appropriate style for the firm.

Presentation to Stardex. In early 1993, Reynolds received a call from an old business acquaintance, Clive Anderson, who was now the assistant treasurer of the Stardex Corporation, a company located in Showcase's community and listed on the New York Stock Exchange. Anderson told Reynolds that Stardex was considering additional managers for $10 million increments of its defined-benefit pension plan and invited him to drop by for a visit to get better acquainted and to discuss the plan.

When Reynolds arrived at the assistant treasurer's office, he faced a three-member search team that asked for very specific information about Showcase investment philosophy, style of management, and performance record. Reynolds realized that he was woefully unprepared for the presentation, so he did some quick improvisations.

Reynolds described the firm's investment approach as client centered, with an eclectic style. He and his partners had not focused on investment returns in their marketing efforts, except in very general terms, so he had no specific record to present. He then remembered the Fund A returns from his association with First National Bank and the good performance of the Taylor account, so he told the search team that Showcase had returns of "about 20 percent a year, with no down years." Anderson and his group were quite impressed by the performance numbers and invited Reynolds to return in two weeks to meet with the entire Stardex Retirement Plan Investment Committee to provide a sharper definition of Showcase's style and specific information on its record.

Reynolds returned to the office with the exciting news that the firm, now with $30 million under management, had the opportunity to expand by one-third. Martin and Younger shared the excitement; all the partners recognized that this opportunity could be critical in assuring the financial viability of Showcase. Martin and Younger, however, were concerned that the 20 percent number for historical performance would be hard to produce in reality.

Younger, like Reynolds, had become a CFA charterholder before the implementation of the AIMR PPS, but she had attended a local financial analysts meeting at which the AIMR PPS were addressed. In discussing how to approach their presentation, Younger recalled that the AIMR PPS encourage the use of composites. So, the Showcase partners decided to use this approach. They remained concerned, however, that even with a composite, they did not have enough years of data to compete for business as important as Stardex's.

Younger recalled from the AIMR PPS discussion that performance may be portable from one firm to another and mentioned this idea to Reynolds. Reynolds offered the use of First National's Fund A because he served on the firm's policy committee that oversaw the fund. Furthermore, Reynolds had been managing the Taylor account since 1986, and its track record, buoyed by Wal-Mart's performance, was terrific. He suggested that they blend the early returns from Fund A with his Taylor account and use them in the composite.

After looking over the record, Younger noted that Reynolds did not invest the $2 million increment to the Taylor account when it was first received in late 1990 because of the recession and the Iraq crisis and that performance had suffered because half of the account was in cash when Operation Desert Storm ignited the great bull market of 1991. That period was so hectic, however, that they decided to assume that the funds came in during mid-1991 when Reynolds began using them.

Younger also pointed out that her value-oriented accounts had performed much better in the past few years than they had previously and that many of these accounts had been beating Reynolds's Taylor account even without the cash adjustment. The three principals agreed that a further blending into the composite of the results of Younger's accounts, although some were balanced accounts and generally very small, would help the composite.

Younger recalled that, according to the AIMR PPS, presenting at least 10 years of data is preferred, but she and Reynolds had only 9 years combined. Then Martin mentioned work that he had done on a model small-cap stock portfolio. Martin had been intrigued by the performance of small-cap stocks, and because the holdings of the two portfolio managers were predominantly in large-cap companies, he had started a small-cap portfolio model in 1992. He had back-tested his model and generated the returns that could have been achieved through a small-cap approach from 1983 through 1992. When the model results were combined with other returns, they not only had 10 years worth of data but also significantly improved overall performance for the composite.

Using these ideas, the partners completed the presentation of the composite performance of Showcase Capital Management in ample time for the meeting with the Stardex investment committee. The performance information was as follows:

Showcase Capital Management: Annual Investment Performance

	1983	1984	1985	1986	1987	1988	1989	1990	1991	1992
Showcase	25.6%	14.8%	23.7%	16.5%	10.4%	21.2%	28.8%	10.1%	32.3%	17.4%
S&P 500	22.5	6.3	32.2	18.5	5.2	16.8	31.5	−3.2	30.5	7.6

As an experienced salesman, Martin knew that the Stardex investment committee would want to determine how well Showcase's returns stacked up against other managers and obtain objective "verification of the good results." Younger remembered that the AIMR PPS also recommend verification of returns. So, Martin provided the Showcase numbers to a friend in the brokerage community whose firm was a consulting group that determined relative performance for the selection of managers for their wrap-fee retail clientele. Martin gave the friend quarterly data for the periods beginning in January 1992 and annualized data for prior years. The results indicated that Showcase was well within the top quartile of the consulting firm's data base.

Armed with this evidence, the three partners put their results in a glossy presentation package for the Stardex committee. The firm's performance numbers are accompanied by the following descriptive wording in a footnote:

The above performance numbers reflect the application of our investment style over a 10-year period. They are taken from a composite of 15 portfolios that aggregate $20 million. The results have been compared with the returns of many other investment advisory firms and have been shown to rank consistently in the top quartile of managers generally. Although no one can foretell the future, we believe, in the words of Patrick Henry, that one can judge the future only in terms of the past.

This report has been prepared and presented in compliance with the Performance Presentation Standards of the Association for Investment Management and Research.

Believing now that they have everything they need, the three principals plan to follow up their meeting with Stardex by reproducing the information about the firm and its performance in a four-color brochure for prospects.

> *What activities at Showcase could be violations of the AIMR Code of Ethics, Standards of Professional Conduct, and Performance Presentation Standards? State what actions the principals of Showcase should have taken or should take to correct the potential violations. Create a general policy statement regarding representation of performance that firms such as Showcase could use to avoid such violations.*

Case Discussion

The partners of Showcase Capital Management have violated the Code, Standards, and AIMR PPS in four areas: improper computation of the composite, erroneous inclusion of past performance data from prior associations, insufficient verification of the data, and improper advertising of the results.

Construction of Investment Performance Composites.
Standard V(B), Performance Presentation, and the elaboration of this standard contained in the AIMR PPS are based on a set of guiding principles that seek to promote full disclosure and fair representation by investment managers of their investment results. The aim of the AIMR PPS is to promote full and fair disclosure of investment returns in a uniform manner so that clients and prospects have sufficient information on which to make decisions relevant to their own circumstances. The founders of Showcase

violated the requirements established to promote the principles in several ways.

▓ *Purpose of composite performance.* Betty Younger was on the right track when she suggested that the firm construct a composite. The AIMR PPS require the use of composites when presenting a firm's performance. The purpose of composites, however, is to demonstrate returns achieved from portfolios or asset classes representing similar strategies or investment objectives. Harvey Reynolds and Younger use different approaches to manage their portfolios, which have compositions that are not highly correlated and results that have been very dissimilar in the past. Indeed, Reynolds's term "eclectic" understates the firm's methodology and style. In shifting from style to style and selecting specific accounts to use, the principals have conspired to present the best returns possible without any intention of portraying actual firm composite returns.

▓ *Composition of composites.* The PPS require that all discretionary fee-paying accounts be included in at least one composite. Furthermore, only assets under the firm's management may be included. The inclusion of investment performance of the First National Equity Common Trust Fund A and the Taylor account that occurred before the existence of Showcase was certainly improper. Although Reynolds sat on the investment policy committee at First National, he did not actually manage Equity Common Trust Fund A and may not use its returns as his own. To use the Taylor account returns, which were dominated by Wal-Mart stock, was also misleading and not representative of most of the accounts Reynolds managed at First National.

When the principals incorporated the results of Fred Martin's small-cap model with actual performance results, they violated the AIMR PPS provisions relating to model portfolios. The AIMR PPS do not preclude the use of and advertising of models, but model returns are not to be linked with the returns of actual portfolios. Model returns must be presented as supplementary information.

The partners also improperly included Mrs. Taylor's $2 million contribution in the calculation of the Taylor account performance used in the composite. The contribution was made in late 1990, but the partners did not include the cash in the calculation of returns until mid-1991. Under the AIMR PPS, all cash contributions must be included in the calculation of performance numbers within the month or quarter that they are received. The AIMR PPS also recommend that when the cash flow exceeds 10 percent of the portfolio's market value, the portfolio be revalued on the date that the cash is received before the calculation of returns.

▓ *Disclosure of composite information.* The principals of Showcase violated several aspects of the AIMR PPS when they omitted certain disclosure requirements related to performance composites. Proper presentation of composites to clients and prospects requires the inclusion of total, time-weighted returns determined at least quarterly, with geometric linking of period returns. Annualized returns must also be presented and should include data from the firm's inception, preferably with a minimum of 10 years. Showcase presented annualized returns for 10 years but included improper accounts, as well as the small-cap model portfolio; model portfolios may not be included. The AIMR PPS require disclosure of the number of portfolios in the composite (unless the number is five or fewer), the total assets in the composite, and the percentage of the firm's clientele represented by the composite. The impact of fees on returns must be documented, and the firm's fee schedule must be disclosed, but Showcase presented neither category.

▪ *Descriptive information.* Although not required, the AIMR PPS recommend that descriptive information be included with composite performance data that will enable prospective clients to understand the risks associated with the returns. Disclosure of the standard deviation of returns of the composite across time as well as the dispersion of returns among participating portfolios is recommended. To demonstrate value added by the managers, the AIMR PPS suggest that benchmark portfolios be constructed that demonstrate returns from an unmanaged portfolio invested in a manner comparable to the firm's. None of this descriptive information was provided by the Showcase principals.

Actions required. If the two portfolio managers could not agree on a common approach, the firm should have prepared two composites to demonstrate the different styles of Reynolds and Younger.

Any composites the firm constructed should have excluded the early results of the Taylor account and those of Fund A. The firm must construct composites of its own accounts. The Taylor account returns do not properly belong in the composite because the disproportionately large holding in Wal-Mart was responsible for the extraordinary returns and that holding was not discretionary; it was retained at the direction of the decedent and his widow, not on the basis of a conscious decision by Reynolds.

The firm must include fully discretionary accounts in at least one of the composites. The small accounts may be excluded, but any exclusions should be uniformly applied.

The returns of the small-cap model portfolio should have been shown separately, with appropriate commentary describing what it represented. It should not have been included in any composite.

The descriptive information required by the AIMR PPS should have accompanied the presentation of the numbers.

Portability of Past Returns. The AIMR PPS take the position that performance records belong to the firm that created them, not to the individuals who were part of the process. Reynolds played a minor part in the establishment of the record achieved by Fund A; at least seven people were involved when he was a section manager and part of the policy committee. Prior to that position, he played no role at all in the fund.

The AIMR PPS do not prohibit disclosure of past returns as long as proper descriptive information is included. The performance must be credited to the prior affiliation, however, and the nature of the manager's position and responsibilities must be detailed. The use of a predecessor's performance could be misleading if one or more individuals other than those at the successor organization played a role in the prior firm's strategy, security selection, or trading. The record may be considered to belong to the firm, however, if a new entity is the product of a change in name or ownership only—that is, if all previous decision makers and substantially all client assets have transferred to the new entity, access to research records remains the same, and the new firm's management has confidence that no misrepresentation will result from presenting the previous firm's record as representing the historical record of the new entity.

In no event is including the past data in the new firm's composite permissible.

Actions required. The firm must construct a new composite. The returns of the Taylor account achieved while at the bank and those of Fund A must be removed from the composite.

Verification by a Third Party. The AIMR PPS recommend but do not require third-party verification of composite returns. The AIMR PPS describe certain minimum procedures that an independent party is required to follow when verifying compliance. In this case, none of those procedures was followed, and even if the procedures had been followed, the firm would not be in compliance.

In addition, the brokerage consulting firm simply accepted Martin's presentation without question. To claim that anyone had checked the data was a misrepresentation.

Actions required. The principals should delete all mention of verification from their new composites.

Compliance with Governing Laws and Regulations. As CFA charterholders, Younger and Reynolds are required to comply with the provisions of the Code and Standards, which include the requirements of Standard I, Fundamental Responsibilities, to know and comply with existing laws and regulations. Neither manager had taken the time to study the requirements of the AIMR PPS relating to the proper presentation of investment performance and the construction of composites. In willfully fabricating and claiming a record that was untrue—both orally at the first meeting with Stardex and in writing—they were violating the antifraud provisions of the Investment Advisers Act of 1940.

The final violation by the principals of Showcase was in the use of a legend advertising compliance with the AIMR PPS. Such a legend may be used only when every reasonable effort has been made to ensure fair, accurate, and complete presentation of performance data and all the requirements of the Standards have been completed.

Actions required. The principals of Showcase should delete any statement that the firm is in compliance until all requirements of the PPS have been fulfilled.

> *Policy statement for a firm.* "Employees shall not make any statements, orally or in writing, that misrepresent the investment performance that they or their firm have accomplished or can be reasonably expected to achieve."

Super Selection

Case Facts

Patricia Cuff, chief financial officer and compliance officer for Super Selection Investment Advisors, has just finished reviewing the brokerage account statement for one of Super Selection's portfolio managers, Karen Trader. When a disgruntled board member of Atlantis Medical Devices (AMD) informed her of Trader's possible misconduct, Cuff decided to investigate Trader's relationship with AMD, a company whose stocks Trader recently bought for all her portfolios. As a result, Cuff obtained and is now reviewing Trader's brokerage statements, which were not previously submitted by Trader. Cuff is concerned about possible violations of the company's standards of professional conduct and her responsibilities as a compliance officer and member of AIMR to act on those violations.

Super Selection is a rapidly growing medium-size money manager registered with the U.S. Securities and Exchange Commission to manage both separate accounts and mutual funds. Super Selection has subscribed to AIMR's Code of Ethics and Standards of Professional Conduct by incorporating the AIMR Code and Standards into the firm's compliance manual. In addition, as an investment advisor to registered mutual funds, Super Selection has incorporated into its code of ethics AIMR's recommendations on personal securities transactions.

Trader has been a portfolio manager for Super Selection for almost five years. She loves the job because of the people she meets and the money she is able to earn. She has been particularly pleased to keep up her friendship with Josey James, a former college classmate and now the president of AMD, a rapidly growing local biotech company.

During the past five years, James has provided Trader with information on attractive stocks in Trader's field—biotechnology—on which Trader capitalized for her Super Selection portfolios and her personal portfolio. Because she was able to act more quickly on her personal trades than her Super Selection trades, Trader has often purchased stocks of the companies recommended by James for her own account prior to purchasing them for her clients. As a result, the performance of her personal portfolio has been better than the performance of her other portfolios.

Three years ago, James asked Trader to serve as an outside director for AMD, and despite AMD's uncertain prospects at the time, Trader eagerly accepted the offer. Because AMD was in shaky financial condition until

This case was written by Paul F. Van Schyndel, CFA, State Street Global Advisors.

recently, the company compensated its directors with stock options rather than cash payments. For the past several years, directors received options exercisable into 200,000 shares in AMD stock. AMD's shares were not traded anywhere, however, so this compensation was essentially worthless and Trader has not reported her relationship with AMD to Super Selection. This year, with AMD's sales setting records and earnings up, directors started receiving quarterly director fees of $5,000.

Several months ago, the AMD board voted to issue shares of stock to the public to raise needed cash. The market for initial public offerings (IPOs) was very hot, with valuations of biotech companies at record levels; so, AMD top managers believed the moment was opportune to go public. A public market for AMD shares was very appealing to many board members. Trader, for example, was eager to exercise her stock options so that she could cash in on their value. She had just begun construction of a new home, which was putting significant pressure on her cash flow. Trader voted, with the majority of the board, to go public as soon as possible—before the new-issue market soured.

Shortly before the public offering date, Trader received a frantic phone call from James asking for a favor. James indicated that the IPO market had reversed course in the preceding few days; valuations of biotech companies were falling rapidly. James was afraid that investor interest in AMD had slowed so much that the IPO was threatened. James asked Trader to commit to purchasing a large amount of the AMD offering for her Super Selection accounts to provide enough support for the offering to proceed as planned.

Trader had previously decided that AMD was a questionable investment for her accounts. As an AMD director, however, she also wanted to see a successful IPO, so she offered to reevaluate that decision. In this reevaluation, AMD's stock price seemed high to Trader. Moreover, if she wanted to achieve the desired volume, AMD stock would then represent a higher percentage of Trader's Super Selection portfolios than most holdings. Nevertheless, Trader decided to purchase the shares as James suggested, and when the IPO was effective, she placed the order for the separate accounts and the mutual funds that she managed.

> *Explain what violations of the Code and Standards have occurred and the steps that Trader should have taken to avoid the violations. What responsibility does Cuff, as compliance officer, have? State what actions Cuff should take now and write short policy statements a firm could use to prevent the violations.*

Case Discussion

Several violations of the Code and Standards have occurred as a result of

Karen Trader's involvement with an outside company, and her personal securities transactions violate U.S. securities laws as well as the Code and Standards.

Trader is neither a CFA charterholder nor a member of AIMR, but she is bound by the AIMR Code and Standards to the extent that they are incorporated in her firm's compliance policies. Patricia Cuff's responsibility to take action regarding violations of the Code and Standards arises from her duties as an AIMR member, as a compliance officer, and as a senior manager of Super Selection.

Responsibilities of Supervisors. Those with legal or compliance responsibilities, such as the designated compliance officer, do not become supervisors solely because they occupy such named positions. Determining supervisory responsibilities depends on a "facts and circumstances test," by which the SEC and the AIMR Standards essentially define a supervisor as a person who has authority to hire, fire, reward, and punish an employee. In this case, even though Trader does not report directly to Cuff, Cuff supervises the actions of all employees of the firm (and has the power to hire, fire, reward, and punish them) in her dual responsibilities as CFO and compliance officer. Therefore, she must comply with Standard III(E), Responsibilities of Supervisors.

As a supervisor, Cuff has a responsibility to take appropriate steps to prevent those she oversees from violating applicable statutes, regulations, or AIMR Standards. As compliance officer, she must also ensure that the firm's policies are being followed and that violations of those policies are addressed.

Actions required. As a supervisor, Cuff should take corrective action after discovering the violations by reporting them to senior management. Cuff and Super Selection's senior managers should then take affirmative steps to ensure that the appropriate action is taken to address the misconduct.

As compliance officer, Cuff should direct or monitor a thorough investigation of Trader's actions, recommend limitations on Trader's activities (such as monitoring all trading done in her client accounts, prohibiting her from personal trading, and imposing sanctions on her, including fines), implement procedures designed to prevent and detect future misconduct, and ensure that her recommendations are carried out.

The senior managers should also consult an attorney to determine whether Trader's actions should be reported to appropriate legal or regulatory bodies. If senior management fails to act, Cuff may need to take additional steps, such as disclosing the incident to Super Selection's board of directors and to the appropriate regulatory authorities, and may need to resign from the firm.

> ***Policy statement for a firm.*** "Employees in a supervisory role are responsible for the actions of the employees they supervise regarding compliance with the firm's policies and procedures and any securities laws and regulations that govern the employees' activities. When supervisors become aware of a violation of securities laws or firm policies, they must notify the compliance officer and senior management and/or ensure that appropriate steps are taken to address the violation."

Employees and the Employer/Supervisor. Trader has responsibilities under Standard III(C), Disclosure of Conflicts to Employer, and Standard III(D), Disclosure of Additional Compensation Arrangements. Trader violated both standards by (1) failing to disclose the conflict of interest that she had as a result of her ownership of Atlantis Medical Devices stock options and (2) failing to disclose to her employer the additional compensation she received as a director of AMD. The stock options and the cash compensation both should have been disclosed.

Actions required. To avoid the violation, Trader should have disclosed to her employer any additional compensation she was receiving, whether cash or any other benefit, and should have disclosed to her supervisor (and her clients) her ownership of the AMD stock options and her directorship. This disclosure would have provided her employer and clients the information necessary to evaluate the objectivity of her investment advice and actions.

Cuff, after discovering the violation, needs to ensure that proper disclosure is made to clients and a thorough review is made of Trader's client accounts and her personal accounts to determine whether any conflicts have occurred in addition to the IPO violation. If conflicts are discovered, Cuff has a responsibility to take appropriate action—e.g., limit behavior, impose sanctions, and so on.

> ***Policy statement for a firm.*** "All personnel are required to inform their supervisors of any outside activities, such as board directorships, in which they are engaged or into which they propose to enter and receive approval for these activities prior to engaging in them. Employees shall disclose all conflicts of interest to clients and the firm prior to engaging in any activity that could be influenced by such conflicts."

Reasonable Basis. Trader had previously determined that AMD was not a suitable investment for her clients. Under pressure from James, Trader has reversed her stance on AMD and has thus violated Standard IV(A.1), Reasonable Basis and Representations.

Actions required. Trader should have diligently and thoroughly researched AMD again prior to making a decision on investing in this security for her clients' accounts. Once having concluded that AMD was not appropriate, she should not change her opinion. Trader must also inform clients of any conflicts she has as an AMD director and as an owner of AMD stock options.

Cuff should periodically—at least annually—review investment actions taken for clients by Super Selection employees to determine whether those actions were taken on a reasonable and adequate basis.

> *Policy statement for a firm.* "Portfolio managers must consider all applicable relevant factors for each investment recommendation. Recommendations should be made in view of client objectives and the basic characteristics of the investment to be bought or sold."

Fiduciary Duty. By investing in and influencing the public offering of AMD in order to boost the price of this stock, Trader misused her professional position for personal benefits and breached her fiduciary duty to her clients, thus violating Standard IV(B.1), Fiduciary Duties.

Although Trader, as a director of AMD, has a duty to that companies' shareholders, she cannot void her obligation to her clients at Super Selection and, in the case situation, should have acted in client interests first.

Actions required. Trader should have taken investment actions that were for the sole benefit of her clients. She should not have been swayed by her ownership of any company into taking an investment action for her clients that she might not have taken in the absence of that ownership.

Cuff must thoroughly investigate Trader's activities to see whether other breaches of fiduciary duty have occurred. Following this type of breach and any others, Cuff must limit the activities of the wrongdoers, ensure the implementation of procedures to prevent and detect future occurrences, and follow up to make sure that her recommendations are carried out.

> *Policy statement for a firm.* "Employees have a responsibility to identify those persons and interests to which they owe a fiduciary duty. Employees must comply with these identified fiduciary duties."

Investment Recommendations and Actions. Trader violated Standard IV(B.2), Portfolio Investment Recommendations and Actions, when she purchased AMD stock for her clients and did not take into consideration their needs and circumstances.

Actions required. Trader should have considered clients' needs and circumstances prior to taking investment actions and should not have taken actions to benefit herself or her friends.

Cuff should establish a periodic review—to occur at least annually—to compare the suitability of investment actions taken for client accounts with the clients' written investment policy statements.

Policy statement for a firm. "The objectives and constraints of each client's portfolio should be put into a written investment policy statement. In taking action or making investment recommendations for clients, employees should consider the needs and circumstances of the client and the basic characteristics of the investment and portfolio involved. No recommendation should be made unless it has been reasonably determined to be suitable for the client's financial situation, investment experience, and objectives."

Priority of Transactions. Trader violated Standard IV(B.4), Priority of Transactions, by trading in close proximity to her clients' trades and may have benefited from the impact of her clients' trades on the stock price. The recommendations of AIMR's Personal Investing Task Force Report, which Super Selection had incorporated in its standards, require duplicate broker confirmations and preclearance on personal trades, but Trader did not follow these procedures.

Actions required. In this instance, Trader circumvented Super Selection's procedures by not reporting trades and brokerage accounts. Nevertheless, Cuff should have made efforts to ensure that Super Selection's policies were being followed. Cuff should review her firm's policies and procedures to make sure they are adequate and determine whether any adjustments should be made to implement or improve them. If adjustments are necessary, she should carry them out.

Cuff should also make sure that employees of Super Selection are periodically informed of the Code and Standards and its requirements so as to eliminate any uncertainty about which employees are covered and what responsibilities they have to comply with these standards.

Cuff needs to investigate Trader's personal transactions thoroughly and recommend appropriate sanctions for Trader's behavior. Cuff must also ensure that her recommended sanctions are followed to completion.

Policy statement for a firm. "The interests of customers will always be given priority over the personal financial interests of the firm's personnel—particularly when securities are being traded or investment actions are being taken.

"All personal trades by employees of the firm will be precleared in accordance with the firm's compliance policies. In addition, personal trades will be monitored for suspicious activity, such as conflicts of interest and trading on material nonpublic information. Any violator of these priority and preclearance policies will be subject to sanctions, including loss of employment."

The Lost Briefcase

Case Facts

Tom Harcourt, a CFA charterholder and member of AIMR, is a senior analyst at Bigelow, Lamont, and Phillips, a major investment banking firm. On a Saturday afternoon, after working all day on a merger proposal for his client, Paramex Medical, Harcourt leaves his office building with his briefcase in hand and witnesses an automobile accident. A pedestrian trips on the sidewalk, falls onto the road, is hit by a car, and is severely injured. Harcourt applies emergency rescue procedures to the victim (saving the person's life) and accompanies the victim to the hospital in an ambulance. In the excitement, Harcourt loses his briefcase.

Bruce Winslow, also a CFA charterholder and member of AIMR, is a portfolio manager with Kramer & Gould, an investment advisory firm serving high-net-worth individuals. He has spent the Saturday afternoon reviewing his client portfolios. About half an hour after the accident, he leaves his office and comes across a briefcase on the sidewalk. The street is deserted. Winslow picks up the briefcase, takes it home with him, opens it, and finds the following:

- notes of an interview with the chief financial officer (CFO) of Paramex Medical, a leading manufacturer of drugs and home medical supplies;
- notes on the financial condition of VitaLifePlus, a national chain of pharmacies and a retailer of health and beauty products;
- a dozen business cards identifying Tom Harcourt, whom Winslow knows because they were classmates and rivals at business school, as the briefcase's owner;
- Harcourt's meeting planner, which shows that he had a three-hour meeting with the Paramex CFO the previous Tuesday, had a four-hour meeting with the president of VitaLifePlus the previous Thursday, and is scheduled to meet them again on the following Tuesday and Thursday, respectively;
- an analysis of Harcourt's personal financial situation showing a net worth of $5 million, $1 million more than Winslow;
- a case of computer diskettes.

Winslow puts the diskettes in his home computer and starts looking through the files. He finds spreadsheets of various pro forma statements

This case was written by Jules Huot, CFA, Pension Commission of Ontario.

and scenarios for a takeover of VitaLifePlus by Paramex Medical. He cannot access one file because it has been encrypted. He copies all these files into his computer.

On Monday morning, Winslow returns Harcourt's briefcase, wrapped in plain brown paper, without any indication of where the parcel has come from. Winslow then puts in orders to buy shares of VitaLifePlus for the accounts of his wife and his mother-in-law. He makes sure that these orders do not exceed 10 percent of the average daily trading volume in VitaLifePlus. These trades take one week to complete, during which the price of the stock does not change materially.

Winslow watches for any news or special announcements concerning Paramex and VitaLifePlus. No news appears, and the price of VitaLifePlus shares remains basically unchanged.

Three months later, VitaLifePlus announces that it will float an issue of high-yield bonds on the market to finance the takeover of Paramex Medical, a takeover it is proposing in order to assure itself of a secure source of capital. The market reacts very badly to this news, and the share price of VitaLifePlus declines by 30 percent in one day.

> *Identify several activities that are or could be violations of the AIMR Code of Ethics and Standards of Professional Conduct. State what Winslow or Harcourt should have done or should do to correct the potential violations, and make a short policy statement firms could use to prevent the violations.*

Case Discussion

This case illustrates how rivalry, envy, and greed can overcome judgment and lead someone to succumb to temptation, break the law, and indulge in unethical conduct. Bruce Winslow and Tom Harcourt are CFA charterholders and members of AIMR, and therefore, they have assumed the responsibility of practicing their profession within the context of the Code and Standards. The case reveals violations of the Code and Standards, however, primarily in the areas of professional misconduct, misappropriation and trading on the basis of material nonpublic information, violation of a client relationship, and noncompliance with securities laws and regulations.

Professional Misconduct. When Winslow rummaged through Harcourt's briefcase, he merely committed an indiscretion, but when he copied Harcourt's computer files, he committed theft of intellectual property. He misappropriated information by reading the documents and the computer files. In so doing, he violated the first tenet of the Code of

Ethics: An AIMR member shall conduct himself or herself with integrity and dignity.

In addition to violating the Code, Winslow violated Standard II(B), Professional Misconduct. The scope of Standard II(B) goes beyond technical compliance with employment-related regulations; it reaches behavior that reflects adversely on the entire investment profession. Standard II(B) states that members shall not commit "any act that reflects adversely on their honesty, trustworthiness, or professional competence." This part of Standard II(B) addresses personal integrity not only as it relates to the reputation of CFA charterholders, CFA candidates, and other AIMR members but also as it reflects on the profession as a whole. It applies to criminal convictions that call a member's honesty and trustworthiness into question.

Standard II(B) also states, "Members shall not engage in any professional conduct involving dishonesty, fraud, deceit, or misrepresentation . . . ." This clause prohibits fraudulent activity and dishonest business schemes, and the provision applies even if the action does not lead to a criminal conviction. Therefore, even if a criminal conviction is avoided (by, for example, the acceptance of a consent decree or the refusal to prosecute), fraud and dishonest schemes violate Standard II(B).

Actions required. Instead of rummaging through the briefcase, Winslow should have limited his examination of it to determining the identity of the owner from the business cards or from the initial pages of Harcourt's diary.

Policy statements for a firm. "All financial analysts and investment professionals shall familiarize themselves with and abide by AIMR's Code of Ethics and Standards of Professional Conduct. They shall comply at all times with all relevant laws and regulations.

"Professional conduct extends beyond legal and regulatory requirements to encompass behavioral and ethical imperatives. Members of the firm shall conduct themselves with integrity and dignity and act in an ethical manner in their dealings with all people— the public, clients, employees, subordinates, and fellow analysts.

"Dishonesty and fraudulent conduct are clearly inconsistent with this requirement and will not be tolerated. These actions will result in sanctions by the Management Committee and may lead to dismissal from the firm."

Use of Material Nonpublic Information. The heart of this case is a violation of Standard V(A), Prohibition against Use of Material Nonpublic Information. In Harcourt's briefcase, Winslow found information about two companies that meets the definition of material nonpublic information—that is, any information about a company or the market for its securities

- that is not generally disclosed to the market and
- the dissemination of which is reasonably certain to affect substantially the market price of those securities or
- that is substantially likely to be considered important by reasonable investors in determining whether to trade in such securities.

How specific the information is, how different it is from public information, what its nature is, and how reliable it is are all important factors in determining the materiality and public nature of the information.

In this case, the identity of the companies is specific. The nature of the deal is not specific; the spreadsheets present different scenarios. The files that Winslow examined did not actually set out terms of a tender offer but could have led a reasonable person to believe, as Winslow evidently did, that preparing the scenarios was a step in a plan designed to lead to an actual offer and that the tender proposal was in the encrypted file. Winslow assumed, based on the source, that the information was reliable, and he traded on it. In this case, therefore, the information was clearly material.

It was also nonpublic; the acquisition scenarios were certainly not known by the public. Therefore, Winslow misappropriated material nonpublic information and used it with the intention of self-gain. He violated his duty under Standard V(A) to disclose or abstain from trading on the basis of inside information.

Trading on or communicating material nonpublic information is illegal; thus, Winslow has not only violated Standard V(A), he has also broken the law and thereby violated Standard I, Fundamental Responsibilities, by failing to comply with governing laws and regulations related to insider trading.

Under the insider-trading provisions of U.S. federal securities law (the Securities Exchange Act of 1934, Rule 10b–5), a trader has a duty to disclose inside information or to abstain from trading on the basis of the information if the trader has a fiduciary or similar relationship of trust and confidence with the corporation whose securities are traded or with its shareholders. Another provision of the Securities Exchange Act (Rule 14e–3) specifically bans trading on the basis of, or communicating inside information about, proposed tender offers. Under the Insider Trading Sanctions Act of 1984, civil monetary penalties can also be imposed on persons buying or selling a security while in possession of material nonpublic information.

Actions required. Winslow should have returned the briefcase to Harcourt personally, advised him of any information that he, Winslow, may have inadvertently seen, and assured him that he would not act on it.

Policy statements for a firm. "Financial analysts, investment professionals, and other members of the firm shall not trade while in possession of material nonpublic information and shall not communicate such information in breach of a duty.

"In addition, personnel shall not misappropriate material nonpublic information, act on it, or communicate it to anyone.

"A financial analyst may also receive nonpublic information from an issuer in the absence of a special or confidential relationship. The analyst should then evaluate its materiality and assess whether the person who communicated the information breached a fiduciary duty. If the information is material and was received through a breach of fiduciary duty, the analyst should make reasonable efforts to achieve public dissemination of the information.

"If the information is not made public, no action shall be taken on the basis of that information and it shall not be communicated to anyone except an employee's supervisor or the firm's compliance officer."

"A financial analyst may receive material nonpublic information in a special or confidential relationship with an issuer and may thereby become a constructive or temporary insider. In such circumstances, the information may be used only for the purpose and in the context in which it was obtained. In that event, the analyst has no need to encourage disclosure of the material nonpublic information.

Confidentiality of Client Information. Harcourt was in a special relationship of trust and confidence—was a constructive insider—with Paramex Medical and VitaLifePlus. He had a duty to preserve the confidentiality of information obtained from the clients and not communicate information about the firms to anyone outside the scope of the special relationship. Harcourt's relationships with both companies meet the two conditions under which confidentiality must be preserved. First, he has a relationship of trust with these parties on the basis of his special ability to conduct a portion of the parties' business. Bigelow, Lamont, and Phillips (and Harcourt) are using their investment banking expertise in advising and planning a takeover of, or merger with, VitaLifePlus by Paramex. Second, the information that Harcourt received resulted from or was relevant to the business that was the subject of the special relationship—Harcourt's facilitation of the projected transaction between these two companies. Harcourt also had an obligation to inform these clients when confidentiality was breached.

Breach of confidentiality. Harcourt's gallant rescue of the pedestrian has, unfortunately, placed him in technical violation of Standard IV(B.5), Preservation of Confidentiality, because he has failed to keep confidential the information communicated to him by his clients.

▓ *Duty of loyalty to clients.* Under Standard IV(B.1), Fiduciary Duties, Harcourt has a duty of loyalty to his clients that requires him to notify them that, as a result of the loss of his briefcase, he failed to preserve the confidentiality of the information given him.

Actions required. Harcourt should have notified his supervisor of the incident, and he and his firm should have sought advice from legal counsel. He and his firm should have apprised Paramex and VitaLifePlus of the incident, presented a status report on the facts known to them, and proposed a contingency plan to preserve the interests of their clients.

Policy statement for a firm. "Personnel charged with acting for the benefit of another person with respect to matters coming within the scope of their relationship with that person are fiduciaries. Financial analysts and other investment professionals shall make every effort to determine applicable fiduciary duties in their relationships with clients, customers, and the firm. They shall fulfill these duties to whom they are owed.

"To comply with this policy, employees should follow at least these steps:

- Observe all laws and rules.
- Investigate fiduciary responsibilities.
- Disclose all conflicts, real or perceived.
- Represent the interests of clients at all times."

FI Investment Management

Case Facts

Jane Bond, CFA, a fixed-income analyst, is pondering her first assignment with FI Investment Management. Bond has been asked to prepare a presentation of the firm's performance record in accordance with the AIMR Performance Presentation Standards (PPS). She is excited by the opportunity to demonstrate her value as a new CFA charterholder through this project.

The Firm. FI Investment Management has $85 million under management in fixed-income securities. Since its inception in 1989, the principals have offered clients a core fixed-income (CF) strategy and a mortgage-backed securities (MBS) strategy. The senior partners, James Stocker and Ann Lender, left a large money management firm in late 1988 to form the new venture, after which they convinced several former clients to follow them. As a result of its excellent returns and tenacious marketing efforts in the early years, FI Investment now has 12 clients.

In the firm's first years of operations, FI Investment's portfolio managers used annual time-weighted total rates of return (including cash and equivalents) and cash-basis accounting to calculate performance. In January 1993, when the partners were able to afford a computerized accounting system, they switched the calculation of performance to quarterly returns with accrual accounting. The firm has always used settlement-date accounting because its clients prefer that practice. FI Investment presents its performance results gross of management fees.

Bond's Performance Table. Bond recalls that the AIMR PPS require portfolios to be grouped by their strategies or investment objectives, so she decides to divide the accounts of FI Investment into two composites. She starts with the CF strategy, which currently has five accounts of $10 million each and two accounts of $5 million each. Bond weights the returns based on the value of each account at the beginning of the quarter; then she links the quarterly returns to create the CF composite annual returns. For the pre-1993 returns, she includes the accounts' returns during the year they signed on as clients, because in those years, the firm was rapidly adding assets from both new and old clients.

One of the large clients, Widdicombe Products, periodically requests that, for tax reasons, FI Investment not realize any gains on Widdicombe's portfolio. Because this restriction rarely lasts for more than a quarter at a

This case was written by Amy F. Lipton, CFA, Bankers Trust.

©*Association for Investment Management and Research*

time and the account's performance has generally been good, Bond decides to include Widdicombe's returns in the CF composite for all periods.

Bond next turns to the MBS portfolios. Until recently, this strategy had six accounts of $5 million each. FI Investment had been terminated by one client, however, Glass Corporation, for poor performance in MBS; so, Bond concentrates on the five remaining accounts, weighting their returns together by account asset size to create the MBS composite.

In order to show a relative measure against which prospective clients can compare the return and risk of FI Investment's portfolios, Bond obtains the returns of the Lehman Aggregate Bond Index. The ABI is an aggregate index of U.S. government and corporate bonds, mortgages, and asset-backed securities. The main index and the many subindexes Lehman Brothers provides are market weighted and composed of investment-grade securities. This market index has an asset allocation and duration similar to the CF strategy. Because she cannot find a pure mortgage index and the ABI has a mortgage-backed securities component, Bond decides to use the ABI also for the MBS strategy.

Bond puts together a table summarizing the annualized returns and durations for the two composites and the index. She remembers to include the number of accounts, assets, and percentage of total assets represented by each composite. She vaguely recalls that portfolio size range is a recommended disclosure. The performance of the $5 million accounts in the CF strategy is inferior to that of the larger accounts, however, and she does not want to call attention to this fact. So she decides not to include this information.

Finally, to comply with AIMR's disclosure requirements, Bond includes the following notes:

- This report has been prepared and presented in compliance with the Performance Presentation Standards of the Association for Investment Management and Research for the period January 1, 1989, through June 30, 1995.
- Results for half-year 1995 are annualized.

> *What activities at FI Investment Management would be violations of the AIMR Code of Ethics and Standards of Professional Conduct? State what actions Bond should take to correct the violations.*

Case Discussion

In this case, the major violations committed by Jane Bond are of AIMR's Performance Presentation Standards and of Standard V(B), Performance Presentation of AIMR's Standards of Professional Conduct. The marketing materials being prepared at the end of the case are leading the firm also into violations of Standard IV(B.6), Prohibition against Misrepresentation of Services.

Standard V(B) requires members to make every effort to assure that performance information is fair, accurate, and complete. If a member intends to meet Standard V(B) by applying the PPS, the member can claim compliance with the PPS only if he or she has made every reasonable effort to assure that such presentation is, in fact, in compliance with the PPS in all material respects.

Compliance with AIMR PPS. In her compilation of performance, Bond incorrectly applied the AIMR PPS in several areas: preparation of composites, mandatory disclosures, recommended guidelines and disclosures, and retroactive compliance.

▨ *Composition of composites.* Bond was correct in splitting the returns of FI Investment Management's assets into two composites in order to reflect the firm's different strategies. In constructing the composites, however, she violated several other requirements of the PPS. Because Widdicombe's tax-related trading restriction may have prevented FI Investment from consistently applying the CF strategy, this account may be considered nondiscretionary. Nondiscretionary accounts should not be included in the preparation of composites.

In addition, the exclusion of Glass Corporation's performance was a violation of the prohibition of "survivor" performance results. The PPS require that terminated accounts be included in composites through the last full period during which they were under management.

Actions required. The Widdicombe account should be excluded from the CF composite because the restriction on trading makes the account nondiscretionary. The Glass account, on the other hand, should be included in the MBS composite for the periods during which it was managed by FI Investment.

▨ *Mandatory disclosures.* Bond omitted two mandatory disclosures required under the PPS relating to the performance table: management fees and settlement-date accounting. Disclosure is required of whether performance is gross or net of investment management fees. In either case, an appropriate schedule of fees must be presented. In addition, the use of settlement-date rather than trade-date accounting must be disclosed.

Actions required. FI Investment must disclose that returns are gross of management fees and must present a fee schedule together with the performance results so that clients in one-on-one presentations can calculate the impact of management fees on potential returns. Additional disclosures may be necessary to satisfy U.S. Securities and Exchange Commission rules regarding advertising performance. Although trade-date accounting is recommended, settlement-date accounting is acceptable; its use, however, must be disclosed.

■ *Recommended guidelines and disclosures.* Bond applied the guidelines and disclosures recommended by the PPS inconsistently. The ABI is a reasonable benchmark for the CF strategy because both the strategy and the benchmark invest across sectors of the U.S. fixed-income market and have similar durations. If a portfolio strategy is different from the benchmark, the PPS recommend that the differences be described. The ABI is not an appropriate benchmark for the MBS strategy, because that strategy invests only in mortgage-backed securities and probably has a shorter duration than the ABI.

Although an external risk measure—duration—is included in the performance table, no internal risk measure, which is recommended by the PPS, is presented. This omission is particularly crucial for a fair representation of FI Investment's results because account size affects portfolio performance in the CF strategy.

Finally, the return for the first half of 1995 was annualized. Although the PPS recommend annualized cumulative performance, they *prohibit* annualization of performance for periods of less than one year.

Actions required. First, FI Investment should use only the mortgage-backed securities component of the ABI as the benchmark for the MBS strategy. Second, to illustrate the effect of account size on portfolio returns, Bond should use a measure of internal risk dispersion, such as asset-weighted standard deviation or a high–low range of returns. At the very least, Bond should include portfolio size range or present an equal-weighted composite for the CF strategy. The first-half 1995 returns must be actual, not annualized, returns.

■ *Retroactive compliance.* Bond's statement that FI Investment is in compliance with the PPS for the period January 1, 1989, through June 30, 1995, is not accurate because the pre-1993 returns are out of compliance; Bond included the returns of new clients in the composites during the year in which the firm began to manage the accounts, not the first full year as required by the PPS. In addition, performance was probably significantly affected by infusions of cash from existing clients during this time, in which case, valuations should have been carried out more frequently than annually to avoid performance distortion.

Actions required. The accounts added during the 1989–92 period should be incorporated in the composites for the first full year under management. To minimize distortions caused by intraperiod cash flows from existing clients, FI Investment could go back and revalue its portfolios more frequently than annually or, if the current record is in compliance but FI chooses not to bring the pre-1993 record into compliance, the firm can link the pre- and post-1993 returns only if it discloses what it is doing and explains the reasons for the pre-1993 noncompliance. Although cash-basis accounting is acceptable for retroactive compliance, FI Investment must also disclose its use, because returns calculated on the cash basis are being linked with returns calculated on an accrual basis.

▨ *Form of performance presentation.* In its current form, the firm's presentation will not represent FI Investment's performance fairly, accurately, or completely. Neither Bond nor the principals have made a reasonable effort to assure compliance, and the presentation violates several aspects of the AIMR PPS; therefore, FI Investment's use of the legend "This report has been prepared and presented in compliance with the Performance Presentation Standards of the Association of Investment Management and Research . . ." is inappropriate.

Actions required. To claim compliance with the PPS, FI Investment must bring its performance table into compliance by implementing the calculations and disclosures previously discussed. Should the firm decide not to adopt the AIMR PPS for the presentation of its performance record, it still must ensure that it is not misrepresenting performance results.

> *Policy statement for a firm.* "The firm will not misrepresent performance. Performance will be presented in accordance with AIMR's Performance Presentation Standards."

Misrepresentation of Services. Bond also violated Standard IV(B)(6), Prohibition against Misrepresentation of Services, by excluding the Glass account from the performance composite results. By excluding an account with poor performance, Bond is misrepresenting returns and thus may be misrepresenting the services that a prospective client might expect to receive.

Actions required. Making the changes previously described in earlier sections will allow FI Investment to reflect accurately the quality of service the firm is able to provide.

The Consultant

Case Facts

Mark Vernley, CFA, is quite disturbed by Plains Pipeline Systems' recent allegation that he has, in essence, acted unethically—the first such accusation in Vernley's career. Although Vernley was exonerated of any allegation of wrongdoing by the authorities, he is worried that his personal reputation and integrity and those of his engineering consulting firm have been damaged. He has decided to make some changes in his personal portfolio and the procedures of the firm to prevent unethical conduct, breaches of the law, or the appearance of improprieties.

Mark Vernley. Vernley, a petroleum engineer with a doctorate in engineering and 30 years of business experience, began his career as a reservoir engineer with Deepwell Explorations. After 15 years with Deepwell, he joined a major brokerage firm as a securities analyst specializing in energy issues. During that time, he acquired his CFA charter and became a member of AIMR. Some eight years later, he set up his own consulting firm, Energetics, Inc., which currently employs 10 professional engineers. Energetics consults on a broad array of projects, including asset and project valuations.

During his years in the investment industry, Vernley invested actively in the stock market (with a concentration in energy stocks). When he worked for Deepwell Explorations, however, he had participated in the employee stock purchase plan and had exercised the stock options granted to him. As a result, a sizable portion of his wealth is now in the shares of Deepwell Explorations. The market value and composition of his current portfolio is as follows:

Deepwell Explorations	$250,000
National Marketing and Refining	50,000
Integrated Energy Resources	45,000
Highridge Oil Pipeline	50,000
Interplains Gas Pipeline	75,000
Logline Well Service	35,000
Subtotal	$505,000
Shares in other industries	475,000
Total portfolio	$980,000

This case was written by Jules A. Huot, CFA, Pension Commission of Ontario.

Vernley's practice during the past seven years has been quite profitable, and business is brisk. His peers generally consider him very successful. He has kept up his membership in AIMR and has taken an active part in energy industry affairs. He is a long-standing member of his local and national professional engineers societies. He has served as president of the local engineers society for several terms and as a member of the society's professional standards committee on the national level. Although he has never written down the professional standards he expects of the company's employees, all of the engineers belong to the professional engineers society and he has made clear in personal communications that he expects them to meet high standards in honesty, fairness, and avoiding conflicts of interest. Vernley himself is known for his professionalism, expertise, and integrity.

The Consulting Contract. Energetics recently won a contract, for which Vernley wrote the proposal, from Highridge Oil Pipeline to devise a plan to resolve conflicts with Highridge's clients. Highridge has a long history of disputes with the users of its pipeline—the shippers of oil—over the tolls charged. Highridge wants to recover increases in its operating costs; the shippers want regulations that reflect the market-driven competitive conditions of the industry. They believe such regulations will force Highridge to increase efficiency in its operations. Both parties have engaged in expensive and acrimonious hearings before the regulatory agency.

Vernley's plan for Highridge consists of an incentive-based method to set pipeline tolls, which would give Highridge a financial incentive to operate its pipeline more economically than at present. Under the plan, Highridge will share with the oil companies, including Deepwell Explorations and Integrated Energy Resources, any increase in earnings that results from reduced costs. The result should lower pipeline tolls, eliminate contentious rate hearings, and increase Highridge's profits.

After lengthy hearings, the regulatory agency ratified this plan. But Plains Pipeline Systems, a consistently more efficient and profitable carrier than Highridge, filed an objection with the regulatory agency to the effect that Vernley's plan was flawed because he had a conflict of interest arising from his personal portfolio positions. At a subsequent hearing, the regulatory agency rejected Plains Pipeline Systems' objection and confirmed its prior decision.

> *Discuss the actions that Vernley could have taken to avoid any allegations of conflict of interest based on his holdings of energy company shares. Create a plan that will enable Vernley to shield his company from unethical acts that his employees might commit.*

Case Discussion

In this case, a professional engineer has been charged with having a conflict of interest that prevented him from offering objective advice to his client. The engineer/owner has spent his entire career in the oil industry and enjoyed an excellent reputation and strong financial success. This allegation is the first of any kind made against him or his firm. It has been dismissed, and he is confident that all his employees are honest and that he can rely on them to act in an ethical and professional manner, something he took for granted until now. He is disturbed, however, about the effect of the allegations on his and his firm's reputation, and he wants to avoid any allegations in the future.

Conflicts of Interest in a Personal Portfolio. Vernley can deal with conflicts of interest in two ways. The ideal is to avoid all conflicts of interest, real or perceived. If a conflict of interest cannot be avoided, however, then full disclosure must be made to the interested parties. Each approach entails various options.

■ *Avoidance.* Vernley can avoid any conflict between the interests of his clients and his personal investments if he refrains from investing in any energy-related securities. Because he already holds a portfolio heavily invested in such stock, the next logical step if he follows this course is divestiture. Selling his investments is a drastic option, however, that Vernley might find unreasonable. After all, he built up his portfolio gradually over the course of his long career when he could not foresee his current situation.

Another option is to establish a "blind trust," in which the account is fully discretionary and the trust beneficiary is not aware of the holdings until they are reported by the manager to the extent required by law, usually on a quarterly basis. To retain his current holdings, Vernley's investment policy might specify that his account hold a certain percentage of energy-related issues. Under this arrangement, Vernley would still know what his holdings are, however, if only after the fact. Although he would not know the exact nature of future transactions in his portfolio, he could reasonably anticipate their general direction (because of the account policies and guidelines). In any event, he could still be perceived as having a conflict, which would require that he disclose it to his clients.

An option that would keep Vernley at arm's length would be to make his oil and gas investments by way of a mutual fund specializing in energy-related issues, which would be managed by a third party over which Vernley would have no influence. In this way, he would share in a portfolio that is likely to be much more diversified than his current portfolio, thereby removing any question of the materiality of any one holding. He would also not take part in any investment decision making.

▓ *Disclosure.* Whenever Vernley has a real or perceived conflict of interest because he holds shares whose prices may change if his clients adopt his recommendations, he must disclose such conflicts to his clients. Disclosure can take many forms, which depend on the circumstances. At a minimum, Vernley must disclose to clients of Energetics the existence and the nature of any conflict of interest surrounding a consulting assignment. Then, it is up to the client to evaluate the materiality of Vernley's beneficial ownership of shares and whether the conflict of interest is significant enough to affect Vernley's ability to give advice or make recommendations that are unbiased and objective.

If, in order to keep his personal matters private, Vernley decides to disclose conflicts to clients only when they are material, he is flirting with danger. Establishing what is material is difficult in any context because of the judgment required. Many people will perceive a conflict of interest no matter what the materiality.

Some Energetics consulting assignments may entail the preparation of a submission to the regulatory agency. In certain circumstances, Energetics would need to disclose in the submission a detailed list of Vernley's holdings. Because these documents are usually in the public domain, such declarations generally constitute public disclosure.

A Plan for Energetics. Nothing in this case suggests that any member of Energetics acted unethically. On the contrary, the description of Vernley's activities, the engineers' affiliations, and the overall reputation of Vernley and his firm lead to the conclusion that ethical values permeate the company, infusing the organization and its operating systems with a self-sustaining ethical culture. Energetics operates in an environment, however, in which the absence of a formal compliance program could expose it to costly liabilities in the event of a mishap. At a minimum, the perception of a potential conflict of interest could place the firm in an unfavorable light in the eyes of its clients.

Vernley needs to establish a comprehensive formal compliance system. The main objectives of the program will be to deter unethical or illegal acts and to provide an "affirmative defense" in the event of employee violations. The fears of being caught and of being punished are prominent enforcement characteristics of compliance systems.

For proper implementation, a compliance program must have a number of features: communication, education, and compliance procedures.

▓ *Communication.* The company must inform employees of the standards to which they must conform and must deliver to employees copies of these standards—whether statutes, codes of conduct, or standards of practice. In this case, Vernley could use the AIMR Code of Ethics and Standards of Professional Conduct as the basis for a formal compliance manual.

     ▒ *Education.* The company must educate employees about the main features of the adopted standards and some of their intricacies through workshops and training sessions. Attendance at these sessions should be compulsory, and the sessions should include case studies to illustrate practical applications of the standards.

     ▒ *Procedures for compliance.* Companies should have written documents that spell out their compliance procedures. A company can document several measures that are aids in managing its compliance program effectively, including

- annual certification by employees that they have maintained familiarity with the standards and agree to abide by them;
- required employee memberships in organizations that maintain standards required for the practice of their professions—for example, continued affiliation by Energetics's engineers with the association of professional engineers.
- for the purpose of detecting conflicts of interest or insider trading, required reporting by employees, at least quarterly, of all securities transactions for their own personal accounts or those in which they have a beneficial interest;
- disclosing to management the existence and nature of any possible or actual compensation from sources other than the employer; and
- certification by employees that they have not entered into an independent business activity in competition with their employer. The purpose of this measure is to protect the firm from, for example, misappropriation of trade secrets, misuse of confidential information, solicitation of customers prior to cessation of employment, or self-dealing.

Culture and Leadership. Vernley should continue instilling an ethical culture in Energetics by developing a corporate credo and moral system based on his and his colleagues' professional standards, self-interest, values, and ideals. The intention is for the system to become a social arrangement among interdependent peers that is grounded in responsible conduct and self-governance according to the chosen values. The essential characteristic of this approach is that the culture be based on the collective integrity of the organization, with its members sharing a set of guiding principles and agreeing to joint accountability.

     This approach recommended for Vernley is leader driven. Leaders gain credibility when they develop and communicate their guiding values, integrate them in their operations, and imbue the company's decision-making processes with them.

Pearl Investment Management (A)

Case Facts

After obtaining an M.B.A. in finance, Peter Sherman is offered a position as an account manager with Pearl Investment Management, an investment counseling firm specializing in equity portfolio management for pension and profit-sharing funds, endowment funds, and high-net-worth individuals' accounts. Sherman begins work in the firm's back office, handling administrative tasks for his assigned accounts, settling transactions, balancing the accounts to bank records, and ensuring that client guidelines are followed.

Pearl is a large firm with a number of different departments, including account administration, research, and portfolio management. Having its own research staff allows Pearl to temper its reliance on brokerage firm research, to weigh its conclusions against the opinions of others, and to perform security analysis on companies that are not well followed for Pearl's proprietary use in client portfolio recommendations.

Many of the portfolio managers and analysts at Pearl are CFA charterholders, and as a result, the firm has adopted the AIMR Code of Ethics and Standards of Professional Conduct as part of its policy for internal compliance. The firm policy manual also contains excerpts from laws and regulations that govern investment advisors such as Pearl (and its employees), including sections from the Securities Act of 1933, the Securities Exchange Act of 1934, the Investment Advisers Act of 1940, and the National Association of Securities Dealers manual. All employees must read and sign a statement when they join the firm that they have read Pearl's policies and must repeat this procedure at the beginning of each subsequent year as a reminder of their compliance responsibilities.

On Sherman's first day on the job, his department head gives him the policy manual as part of his orientation program, requests that he read it during the day before signing the compliance statement, and advises him that the firm's Compliance Department will answer any questions he may have. Sherman reads through the manual quickly and then signs the company's personnel policies statement.

After a few months, Sherman feels comfortable handling the administrative

This case was written by Glen A. Holden, Jr., CFA, The Capitol Life Insurance Company.

tasks related to the client accounts he manages at Pearl and ensuring that client investment guidelines are being followed. He enjoys the challenges of being the account manager for his (and Pearl's) clients, the close access to investment information and strategies, and the opportunity to invest his savings with greater insight and understanding than he had before this job. Previously, his personal investments had been in no-load mutual funds, but in his new position, he sees that he can achieve greater reward by building a portfolio of his own.

To further this goal, Sherman reads books about investments and portfolio strategy, as well as the company summaries generated by the firm's Research Department, and he follows the daily price changes of the firm's major holdings. He enjoys discussing his new-found knowledge with family and friends. To put his new knowledge to work in his own portfolio, Sherman decides to open an account with a national discount broker and purchase a few of the stocks that are Pearl's largest equity positions.

> *Identify violations or possible violations of the AIMR Code and Standards in this case, state what actions are required by Sherman and/or his supervisor to correct the potential violations, and make a short policy statement a firm could use to prevent the violations.*

Case Discussion

This case illustrates how easily a young, unwary analyst can slip into questionable actions. The potential violations evident in this case relate to the responsibilities of supervisors, the obligation to obey all laws and regulations, the standards for trading for personal accounts, and the prohibition against conveying confidential client information.

Fundamental Responsibilities. Under the Code and Standards, the basis for Pearl's policy manual, Peter Sherman, his supervisor, and all employees at Pearl have certain fundamental responsibilities.

▓ *Governing laws and regulations.* Under Part A of Standard I, Fundamental Responsibilities, Sherman is required to know about the laws and regulations governing his behavior and that of the firm. Allusions in the case to Sherman's use of information gained through employment at Pearl indicate that Sherman is not aware of all the regulations governing his behavior. Sherman is in a junior position, however, and the responsibility for educating junior employees generally lies with their supervisors. In a large firm such as Pearl, the Compliance Department, in addition to the supervisor's training, should offer instruction and education in this critical area.

▓ *Legal and ethical violations.* For supervisors, top managers, or any employees to knowingly participate in or assist in a violation of the

Code and Standards gives rise to a violation of Part B of Standard I. The requirement "knowingly" is important: Although members are presumed to know all applicable laws, rules, and regulations, they may not recognize violations if they are not aware of all the facts giving rise to the violations.

> *Policy statement for a firm.* "Employees shall maintain knowledge of and comply with all applicable laws, rules, or regulations, including the firm's code of ethics and compliance procedures. Employees shall not knowingly participate or assist in any violation of such laws, rules, or regulations."

Responsibilities of Supervisors. Under Standard III(E), Responsibilities of Supervisors, those in a supervisory position must establish *and implement* internal compliance procedures. AIMR members who act in supervisory roles are expected to understand what constitutes an adequate compliance system for the firm and to make reasonable efforts to see that appropriate procedures are established, documented, and communicated to covered personnel and to the legal, compliance, and auditing departments. The facts that Pearl has a compliance manual as part of the employee handbook and that compliance is monitored by the Compliance Department do not release Sherman's department head from his supervisory duty.

Actions required. A supervisor must take steps to ensure that the compliance procedures are adequate and followed by the employees they supervise. Sherman's supervisor should have reviewed the contents of the compliance manual with Sherman when he was hired and answered any of Sherman's questions or concerns. The supervisor should have also monitored all Sherman's actions to ensure that he was following the firm's policies.

> *Policy statement for a firm.* "Supervisors shall exercise reasonable supervision over those employees subject to their control and shall monitor all actions of employees in their charge to determine that the firm's policies are being followed and to prevent any violation by such persons of applicable statutes, regulations, or provisions of the Code of Ethics and Standards of Professional Conduct.
>
> "Supervisors shall review the contents of the compliance manual with all direct charges when they are hired and answer any questions or concerns the employees may have."

Trading in Client Securities for Personal Accounts. Sherman may be trading in securities that the portfolio managers are purchasing (or selling) for the firm's client accounts and, in doing so, may be violating Standard IV(B.3), Fair Dealing, and Standard IV(B.4), Priority of Transactions. (Members also must not engage in trading ahead of the dissemination of research reports or investment recommendations to clients—a practice that creates a conflict with members' duties to clients). The mutual funds that Sherman used previously would not violate these provisions because Sherman would not be privy to the mutual fund managers' investment actions or security selections. Now, any change in Sherman's investment strategy may well be a result of gaining proprietary information from Pearl. Under the Code and Standards, Sherman may not invest in the same or related securities for his personal account using proprietary information communicated to him in the course of his job in advance of such information being given to all the firm's clients or in advance of client trades. This restriction includes both Sherman's personal account and any other related account in which Sherman has a beneficial ownership (i.e., a direct or indirect pecuniary interest). Personal trades under the Code and Standards must come after those for client portfolios; whether or not the employee is restricted from trading for some specified period of time—such as the 24-hour restriction recommended by AIMR's Personal Investing Task Force (see the topical study titled "Personal Investing" in the *Standards of Practice Handbook*)—securities trading for client portfolios *always* has priority over personal trades.

Actions required. Before placing orders related to individual securities for his own account, Sherman should submit these plans to the Compliance Department for confirmation that his actions will not interfere with or take priority over client transactions.

> *Policy statement for a firm.* "Employees shall submit personal trades to the Compliance Department for approval in advance of any personal investment action in order to clear the trades against client transactions. In the event that an employee wishes to transact in securities that are being traded for clients, the employee will be allowed to trade only after all client transactions have been processed, the Compliance Department has approved the request, and the 24-hour moratorium has expired. On a monthly basis, all personal trades (as shown on brokerage statements of account) must be submitted to the Compliance Department for review."

Conveying Confidential Client Information. Sherman has a duty to see that the proprietary nature of Pearl's investment strategy is maintained and not communicated in the course of his investment activities. The fact that Sherman enjoys discussing his "new-found knowledge" with friends and family suggests a potential violation under Standard IV(B.1), Fiduciary Duties, and Standard III(B), Duty to Employer. Because of his relationship of special trust, Sherman is obligated to take care that he communicates no information that would breach this trust. This obligation is in force whether or not he acts on the information himself.

Actions required. Sherman must take care not to divulge specific investment actions or information exclusive to client relationships that breach his fiduciary duty to the firm and its clients. When in doubt, Sherman should request guidance from the Compliance Department.

Policy statement for a firm. "Proprietary information shall not be communicated outside the firm. 'Proprietary' includes information about client portfolios, investment strategies, and portfolio actions and recommendations. Furthermore, employees should be mindful of the special relationship with Pearl's clients and ensure that the highest degree of care is preserved when investment action is taken on their behalf."

Pearl Investment Management (B)

Case Facts

Competition for the infrequent job openings at Pearl Investment Management is extensive, both from within the firm and from the outside. After a year in Pearl's back office as one of the account managers, Peter Sherman is told that obtaining a CFA charter would greatly enhance his chances of moving into the firm's research area. Sherman studies at length and passes Level I of the CFA exam.

In the next year, Sherman is helpful in clearing up problems related to the allocation of block trades among certain large client accounts. The most difficult problem is a misallocation related to an initial public offering (IPO) of Gene Alteration Research Corporation. Sherman was assigned this project because of his accounting experience and because none of his client portfolios was involved, although most of his institutional accounts and a few of his larger individual accounts are "total rate of return" portfolios.

Because his review is a rush project, Sherman does not have time to consult the clients' investment policy statements, but he feels certain that the portfolio managers would direct only suitable trades to their client accounts. Furthermore, he believes the Trading Desk would have acted as a second review for client investment guidelines. Sherman reconciles the transactions related to the block trades across all the portfolios in question. As a result, certain securities are shifted among accounts. Sherman believes that with the adjustments and with the transactions reversed and reallocated at the IPO price for the Gene Alteration issue, all clients have been treated fairly, but he wonders how the problems arose in the first place.

> *Several activities at Pearl are or could be in violation of the Code of Ethics and Standards of Professional Conduct. Identify violations and possible violations, state what actions are required by Sherman and/or the firm to correct the potential violations, and make a short policy statement a firm could use to prevent the violations.*

This case was written by Glen A. Holden, Jr., CFA, The Capitol Life Insurance Company.

Case Discussion

The pressure of a rush project assigned by one's bosses and faulty assumptions can lead to inappropriate shortcuts even when intentions are good. This case involves violations or potential violations of the CFA candidate's compliance responsibility, fair dealing with clients, fiduciary duty to clients, appropriateness or suitability of investment recommendations or investment action, and correction of trading errors in client accounts.

Responsibility of Candidates to Comply with the Code and Standards. As an employee, Sherman was bound only by Pearl's own personnel policies. As a CFA candidate, he is subject to the Code and the Standards, and he must rely more on his own knowledge of the Code and Standards to maintain compliance, with assistance from Pearl's Compliance Department, than on company explanations of the Code and Standards. As a CFA candidate, Sherman is now subject to disciplinary action by AIMR for violations of the Code and Standards, whether or not Pearl takes action. Because Pearl has incorporated the AIMR Code and Standards into its personnel policies, Sherman is relieved of his duty under Standard III(A), Obligation to Inform Employer of Code and Standards, to give formal notification of his obligations.

Actions required. Sherman should reacquaint himself with Pearl's personnel policies and read through the AIMR *Standards of Practice Handbook* to increase his familiarity with the Code and Standards and the subtleties of implementing the Standards on a day-to-day basis. The detailed discussion of Standards and examples in the *Handbook* provide explanations and add depth to the meanings of the various Standards. Finally, to be safe, Sherman should document for his supervisor that, as a CFA candidate, he is obligated to comply with AIMR's Code and Standards and that he is subject to disciplinary sanctions for violations thereof.

Dealing with Clients. The case presents evidence of failure by Pearl Investment Management and its employees to carry out their fiduciary duties and their obligation to treat all clients equitably.

    ▪ *Fiduciary duty.* Standard IV(B.1), Fiduciary Duties, requires members to take investment actions for the sole benefit of the client and in the best interest of the client *given the known facts and circumstances.* In other words, fiduciaries must manage any pool of assets in their control in accordance with the needs and circumstances of clients. The case notes that Sherman did not consult the clients' investment policy statements, however, when reallocating the IPO trades. He assumed the portfolio managers and/or the Trading Desk would have done so. Therefore, Sherman violated his fiduciary duties by not making sure that the reallocations were in the best interests of all clients and suitable to each client.

    ▓ *Fair dealing*. In allocating or reallocating block trades, a member must ensure that Standard IV(B.3), Fair Dealing, is upheld. The case notes that among the problems Sherman was asked to review was allocation of an IPO "among certain large client accounts." By favoring their large client accounts over others with similar investment objectives, the portfolio managers, the Trading Desk, and the account managers involved violated AIMR's and Pearl's standards on fair dealing.

    Members have a duty to treat all clients *fairly* so that no one client is advantaged or disadvantaged—no matter what the size of the portfolio or other qualifications. Clients' investment guidelines often differ significantly, however, so portfolio managers and the Trading Desk must determine, in advance, which accounts have similar investment objectives and should receive similar allocations when new purchases are made. Even if clients have identical investment objectives, the accounts may have different cash reserves, dissimilar inclinations toward leverage through the use of margin, and distinct minimums for transaction size. All these factors must be taken into account in the decision-making process.

    Ultimately, however, Pearl should treat portfolios with similar investment objectives and constraints similarly regardless of the size of the portfolios or the fees that they convey to Pearl. In making new securities purchases, firms should allocate a purchase for all suitable accounts, using a pro rata or similar system of distribution when less than the full order is received.

Actions required. Sherman must re-investigate the investment objectives for all affected client portfolios to make certain that orders were not entered in violation of client guidelines. He must also ensure that the allocation of block trades is made on an equitable basis for *all* client portfolios of similar objectives; in carrying out this assignment, he must keep in mind minimum transaction size but include all accounts that have similar investment criteria.

    Policy statements for a firm. "Employees owe a fiduciary duty to clients, and in all instances, the interests of clients shall come first. Action contrary to this policy is expressly prohibited.

    "Allocation of trades shall be on a fair and equitable basis for all portfolios with similar investment objectives and constraints."

Bearing the Financial Risk of Errors in Client Accounts.

When trades are made in error or are misallocated, under no circumstance should client portfolios bear the risk of an inappropriate transaction; nor should the firm shift the burden to another portfolio or client account. The burden or financial risk must be absorbed by the firm, not by the client (either directly or indirectly).

The reversal of trades described in the case and the reallocation of securities at the IPO price comes close to being a complete resolution of the problem Sherman was asked to solve, but Pearl should have credited short-term interest to those accounts from which transactions were removed because the clients' cash accounts were used to cover the trades.

In some instances, investment management firms shift financial risk to a client (or clients) indirectly by using such techniques as letting soft-dollar trades "cover" the financial aspects of a reversal, canceling an order through a "sale" from one account and a coincident "repurchase" in another account, or other transactions to compensate the firm for any loss it incurred by transacting at levels different from the market. Many client portfolios may be involved in order to spread the financial effects over a broad number of portfolios, which complicates the firm's or the manager's efforts to discern this ethical infraction. Any activity of this sort is a violation of AIMR's Code and Standards related to fair dealing and fiduciary duty.

Actions required. Pearl should see that no client bears a financial loss by the misallocation of block trades by any Pearl employee. As compensation for the use of the clients' funds, Pearl should credit short-term interest to all accounts for which trades were reversed, with Pearl bearing the loss. Short-term interest should *not* be charged against accounts that received shares.

> *Policy statement for a firm.* "The firm will take all steps necessary to ensure the integrity of its client accounts. When errors do occur, the clients' portfolios will be restored with no loss of value to the client. To the extent that such losses occur, Pearl will indemnify its clients and make the appropriate restitution."

Pearl Investment Management (C)

Case Facts

After Peter Sherman passed Level II of the CFA exam, Tomas Champa, Pearl Investment Management's director of research, requested that Sherman be transferred to the Research Department with the understanding that his apprenticeship in the department as a junior analyst would last at least until he was awarded the CFA charter. Sherman was thrilled at the prospect of moving into research, and he accepted the transfer.

Champa came to Pearl when he decided to remain in the United States after completing a 5-year U.S. tour of duty for a major international bank with which he had served for 20 years. His background in international banking has made him particularly well suited to be the research director at Pearl. Champa has seven analysts in his department—five senior analysts and two junior analysts. Sherman is one junior analyst, and the other is a Level III CFA candidate.

Champa is anxious to lead the firm's research efforts into international securities and wants to begin with companies in the developing countries whose markets have experienced spectacular performance in recent years. He tells the analysts that Pearl must come up with research recommendations in emerging market equities quickly or the department will face criticism from senior management and the firm's clients. He also wants to be able to attract prospective clients by demonstrating the firm's expertise in this area.

Although Sherman is new to the department, Champa gives him difficult assignments because he believes Sherman's lack of preconceived notions about emerging market companies makes him an ideal analyst for this area. Sherman is to concentrate on Central and South America, areas where Champa believes he has special insight and can direct Sherman.

Sherman reads several brokerage reports on Latin American markets, spends time with Champa and other members of the Research Department discussing trends in these markets, and browses through the statistical section of Standard & Poor's *International Stock Guide*. For a briefing by someone with actual experience, Champa refers Sherman to one of his old banking contacts, Gonzalo Alves, who is well connected in Mexico and on the board of directors of a number of important Mexican corporations.

This case was written by Glen A. Holden, Jr., CFA, The Capitol Life Insurance Company.

Sherman spends several hours speaking with Alves about the Mexican economy and the companies for which Alves serves as a director. Alves tells Sherman about the strategic direction of each company, some potential acquisition targets, and how changes in the Mexican economy will affect each company directly. Sherman now feels comfortable using this information in writing his research reports.

Champa asks Sherman to produce a research report on several Mexican telecommunications and cable companies. Because of the deadline Champa gives Sherman for the report, Sherman cannot develop the research easily on his own, so he plans to incorporate information from his reading of the brokerage firm reports, his conversation with Alves, and other sources. Sherman hastily finishes his two-page report, "Telecommunications Companies in Mexico," which includes excerpts from the brokerage reports, general trends and ratios from the S&P *International Stock Guide,* and paraphrased opinions from Alves. It concludes with an internal recommendation that stock in the Mexican telecommunications companies be bought for Pearl clients for which such stock is suitable. Sherman does not cite the brokerage reports as sources because they are so widely distributed in the investment community.

Pearl's senior managers applaud Champa and his staff for their quick response to the market demand for emerging market research, and the portfolio managers ask the Research Department for more recommendations. Jill Grant, however, the other junior research analyst, asks Sherman why his report did not include specific details about the Mexican economy or the historical exchange rate fluctuations between the Mexican peso and the U.S. dollar. She questions the comparability of Mexican securities with U.S. securities and notes that the diversification available from investing in global markets is achieved only if the correlation between the specific non-U.S. market and the U.S. market is low. Sherman's response, supported by Champa, is, "Our clients are sophisticated investors; they know these things already."

> *The case reveals several activities at Pearl that are or could be in violation of the AIMR Code of Ethics and Standards of Professional Conduct. Identify violations and possible violations, state what actions are required by Sherman or his supervisor to correct the potential violations, and make a short policy statement a firm could use to prevent the violations.*

Case Discussion

The pressures to succeed can lead to noncompliance in ordinary, mundane business activities. The violations or potential violations in this case relate to using proper care and independent judgment, use of insider information (particularly under international applications of the Code and Standards and the obligation of members to comply with governing laws and regulations), several aspects of research and research reports, and representation of services.

Proper Care and Independent Judgment. The final requirement stipulated in the AIMR Code of Ethics is to use proper care and exercise independent professional judgment. When Peter Sherman succumbed to the time pressures exerted by Tomas Champa, he was thus violating a basic provision of the Code and Standard IV(A.3), Independence and Objectivity.

Actions required. Sherman must keep in mind the necessary steps in the research and portfolio decision-making process and resist attempts to rush his analysis.

> *Policy statement for a firm.* "Analysts shall use proper care and exercise independent professional judgment in the preparation of research reports to ensure that reports are thorough, are accurate, and include all relevant factors."

Use of Insider Information. Sherman must base any investment recommendations on his research alone, without incorporating material nonpublic information and without engaging in illegal or unethical actions. The situation in which Sherman found himself discussing a number of important corporations with Alves was compromising at best. Based on the local laws and customs with which they were most familiar, Champa and Alves may have found a candid discussion about the corporations where Alves served in a close relationship to be perfectly acceptable. In the course of conversation, however, Alves could have conveyed material nonpublic information to Sherman. If Sherman used such material nonpublic information in his report, which contained recommendations for investment actions, he violated Standard V(A), Prohibition against Use of Material Nonpublic Information.

One of the more difficult aspects for members is reconciling their obligations under the Code and Standards with the different laws, rules, regulations, and customs of various countries. CFA charterholders, CFA candidates, and AIMR members are held to the highest standards. Therefore, regardless of local laws, they are obligated by the Code and the Standards to refrain from using confidential information to their advantage or the advantage of their clients.

Being compelled to hold to a higher standard than the local norm can be disadvantageous to CFA charterholders and, sometimes, their clients and customers. The higher standard, however, is what sets CFA charterholders apart in terms of the integrity of the investment profession.

Champa's referral of Sherman to Alves can aid Sherman in his research, but Sherman must use the information in an ethical manner. A consideration of the "mosaic theory" can add a useful perspective to judging proper and improper use of information. The mosaic theory states that a compilation of information that is *not material* or is *public* is not a violation of the Standards; it is the result of good analytical work. For example, if Sherman is doing a thorough review and analysis of all companies within a specific sector or industry, he may develop a greater sense of the interrelationships among the companies than if he were studying only one or a few of them. In that case, Sherman may be able, based on public information gathered from a variety of sources *and* his unique understanding, to form conclusions about a particular company that may appear to be based on nonpublic information but are not.

Actions required. Sherman may not use material nonpublic information to take investment action or provide investment advice. If Sherman has come into possession of material nonpublic information in his contact with Alves, he must disclose this fact to Pearl's Compliance Department or compliance officer.

> *Policy statement for a firm.* "Analysts and portfolio managers are prohibited from using material nonpublic information in any form in making investment recommendations or taking investment action. Any employees who have come into possession of material nonpublic information (or who believe they have) shall contact the Compliance Department or compliance officer for guidance. If the information is determined to be material nonpublic information, the employee must refrain from acting on it and should take steps to have the information disseminated publicly."

Using the Research of Others. Sherman's research reports must acknowledge and give credit to the research of others unless the information is of a statistical nature and widely held to be in the public domain. The case says that Sherman did "not cite the brokerage reports as sources because they are so widely distributed in the investment community." To use the proprietary research of others—brokerage reports, for example—without giving them due credit is a violation of Standard II(C), Prohibition against Plagiarism. Sherman's use of general trends and ratios from the S&P *International Stock Guide,* however, is a perfectly legitimate use of information widely available in the public domain.

Actions required. In order to avoid an ethical violation, Sherman must acknowledge the use of someone else's information and must identify its author or publisher. In particular, Sherman must give credit to the author(s) of any brokerage reports he uses extensively in the preparation of internal recommendations.

> *Policy statement for a firm.* "Analysts are prohibited from using the work of others without reference and are prohibited from plagiarizing the work of others by not giving due credit to the author, whether or not the author is employed by the firm."

Reasonable Basis for a Research Opinion. Standard IV (A.1), Reasonable Basis and Representations, requires Sherman to "exercise diligence and thoroughness in making investment recommendations," "have a reasonable and adequate basis" for such recommendations, and "avoid any material misrepresentation in any . . . investment recommendation." Sherman's lack of care and independent research in the preparation of his report is a violation of Standard IV(A.1).

Sherman was essentially taking over the recommendations of others, which may or may not have had a reasonable basis. The research he used may have incorporated material misrepresentations that he did not identify or correct. By copying the work and ideas of others, Sherman may have been copying serious deficiencies and attaching his name and approval to them.

Because of the time pressure from Champa, Sherman did not adequately review the entire industry in the context of the overall economy and global markets (as evidenced by Jill Grant's questions). His reliance on a few brokerage firm reports and other sources is not sufficient to be considered, in the words of Standard IV(A.1), "appropriate research and investigation." Furthermore, his report lacks documentation, not only in detail, but also in substance.

Relevant Factors and Fact versus Opinion in Research Reports. Grant was right to question the exclusion of relevant and basic risk factors in Sherman's report. Sherman has an obligation under Standard IV(A.2), Research Reports, to "use reasonable judgment regarding the inclusion or exclusion of relevant factors in research reports." By excluding important factors, he shirked his responsibility to the firm's clients and violated Standard IV(A.2). Champa's contention that the firm's clients are sophisticated investors who are aware of the characteristics of markets and particular investments does not relieve Sherman of his duty to include relevant factors in his research report.

Actions required. Sherman's reports should be as thorough as possible. When dealing with markets and economies that are significantly different from domestic markets and economies, Sherman should provide a full explanation. The research reports should provide a reasonable basis for decisions, include all relevant factors that reasonably come into play in an investment recommendation, and avoid material misrepresentation of investment characteristics so that the appropriateness of investments for various clients can be judged. Sherman also must maintain records to support his research reports.

> *Policy statement for a firm.* "All relevant factors, including the basic characteristics involved in the investment, are to be included in a research report, with a corresponding discussion of the potential risks involved."

Misrepresentation of Services and Performance Presentation.

The case raises the issue of potential violations of Standard IV(B.6), Prohibition against Misrepresentation. Whether violations are actual would depend, of course, on how the firm's current and prospective clients are made aware of the qualifications of the firm and the Research Department's experience in emerging markets. If Pearl's research is represented as a reaction to a changing marketplace and the increased globalization of securities markets, no violation has occurred. If Pearl is actively soliciting new and existing clients based on its "expertise" in the research and management of emerging market portfolios, however, then a violation of Standard IV(B.6) has occurred.

The presentation of performance—that is, actual investment returns for its emerging market strategy—will be problematic for Pearl in the beginning. Pearl will not be able to report actual performance until it begins to manage portfolios made up of emerging market securities or portfolios that include some meaningful concentration of securities from emerging markets.

Actions required. Pearl must not hold itself out as having experience or any "track record" in the management of emerging market portfolios until it actually manages assets in this area. It can suggest to clients, however, that the qualifications of the firm as demonstrated by its current efforts *might* produce returns that are comparable in a different environment because of the use of a similar methodology.

> *Policy statement for a firm.* "Employees shall make only those statements, either verbally or in writing, about the firm and its qualifications that represent the firm properly and with the integrity it has tried to achieve.
>
> "The firm shall not solicit clients, new or existing, for a new investment style without full disclosure of the firm's qualifications and expectations for both risk and potential return.
>
> "Performance results for a new investment style will be in compliance with Standard V(B), Performance Presentation, as discussed in the AIMR *Standards of Practice Handbook*."

The Glenarm Company

Case Facts

Peter Sherman, CFA, recently joined the Glenarm Company after five years at Pearl Investment Management. He is very excited about the new job and believes he will make a big contribution to Glenarm. His first task is to identify attractive Latin American companies for Glenarm's emerging markets portfolio. Sherman, knowing many of these companies through his consulting contacts, approaches the task enthusiastically. He believes the Glenarm Company will clearly benefit from his knowledge about these companies and has no need to know about his consulting on the side.

Sherman's Background. Sherman joined Pearl Investment Management, a small equity-oriented firm, as a junior research analyst. Pearl entered the international investing arena shortly after Sherman arrived, and Sherman performed well as he gained experience, particularly in researching emerging market securities. Sherman also spent some time handling client relations in the account administration department. More than a year ago, Sherman earned his CFA designation.

Sherman's role at Pearl grew when several of his boss's foreign investment banking contacts hired Pearl to research companies and industries in Latin America in order to better position themselves vis-à-vis their local competitors. When Pearl expanded its research department to accommodate these new projects, the company made Sherman its primary analyst for emerging markets. The firm encouraged Sherman to develop expertise in this area, and he capitalized on his position by serving as a consultant to several third-world companies to assist them in attracting U.S. and European investors, an arrangement that Sherman fully disclosed to Pearl. Pearl did not own stock in any of the companies that Sherman consulted with.

Shortly after Sherman's research responsibilities at Pearl expanded, he received a call from John Lawrence, an acquaintance in the local AIMR financial analysts society and a partner of the Glenarm Company, one of Pearl's competitors. Lawrence indicated that his company was looking for an individual with Sherman's background and asked him if he would be interested in becoming a portfolio manager at Glenarm.

Glenarm. The Glenarm Company is a small equity-oriented manage-

This case was written by Glen A. Holden, Jr., CFA, Capitol Life Insurance Company.

ment firm. Glenarm was recently investigated, censured, and fined by the U.S. Securities and Exchange Commission for a number of violations related to its portfolio management practices. The latest censure was Glenarm's third in the past 13 years. The firm's partners are desperate to rehabilitate their reputation and stem the steady outflow of clients.

No one in the firm other than Lawrence is a member of AIMR, but the Glenarm partners have accepted Lawrence's reasoning that hiring a CFA charterholder as a portfolio manager will enhance the credentials of the firm, will demonstrate a commitment to professionalism in their practice, and is their best chance to expand their client base. Lawrence believes Sherman is an excellent prospect.

The Glenarm partners believe Sherman may be able to bring some business with him if he joins the firm. While at Pearl, Sherman developed client contacts through his duties with the research department and through handling client relations. He also has some knowledge of investment management clients by virtue of his interaction with the portfolio managers. To entice him, Glenarm offers Sherman a large portion of the first-year investment management fee for all the Pearl clients he is able to solicit and bring to Glenarm. Although he has reservations because of Glenarm's past problems with the SEC, Sherman decides that the opportunity is too good to pass up. Also, he can continue his consulting work. So, he agrees to join Glenarm as a portfolio manager.

The Transition. In preparation for his move to Glenarm but while he is still at Pearl, Sherman pays social calls on several local Pearl clients after business hours to inform them that he will be leaving Pearl and encourage them to switch their accounts to Glenarm. He also contacts a number of accounts that Pearl has been actively soliciting but that have not yet committed to hire Pearl as their investment manager and also contacts prospects that Pearl has rejected in the past as too small or incompatible with the firm's business to determine if they are interested in hiring Glenarm. As a result of this activity, Sherman convinces several of Pearl's clients and prospects to hire Glenarm as their investment management company but to delay any action until he has joined Glenarm.

In his last week at Pearl, Sherman identifies material that he has worked on to take with him to his new job, including

- sample marketing presentations he prepared,
- computer program models for stock selection and asset allocation that he developed,
- research material on several companies Sherman has been following,
- news articles he collected that contain potential research ideas, and
- a list of companies that Sherman suggested in the past deserved further

research and possible investment and that were rejected by Pearl.

Several activities in the case are or could be in violation of the Code of Ethics and Standards of Professional Conduct. Identify possible violations and state what actions are required by Sherman and/or Glenarm to correct the potential violations, and make a short policy statement a firm could use to prevent the violations.

Case Discussion

This case depicts violations or possible violations of AIMR's Code and Standards related to a member's duties toward the member's employer: the duty to inform one's employer of the Code and Standards, the duty to disclose to one's employer additional compensation arrangements, and the duty to disclose conflicts of interest to the employer.

Informing the Employer of the Code and Standards. Under Standard III(A), Obligation to Inform Employer of Code and Standards, AIMR members have an obligation to (1) inform their employer, through their direct supervisor, that they are obligated to comply with the Code and Standards and are subject to disciplinary sanctions for violations thereof and (2) deliver a copy of the Code and Standards to their employer if the employer does not have a copy. Technically, Standard III(A) applies to current employers, but members should also keep this obligation in mind as they consider new employment because an obvious implication of Standard III(A) is that members should not accept employment in situations that will not allow them to adhere to their obligations under the Code and Standards.

Peter Sherman was in the difficult situation of trying to weigh a desire for a position that would advance his career against the possibly unethical and unprofessional character of the firm seeking to hire him. The Glenarm Company's checkered history is a red flag signaling potential conflicts between practices at Glenarm and the Code and Standards to which Sherman is committed. Sherman should have made an effort to learn about Glenarm and the individuals working in the firm in advance of making any decision to join the firm. He should have been particularly cautious about considering employment with a disreputable firm because such an association can attract the scrutiny of AIMR's Professional Conduct Program and cause permanent harm to Sherman's professional reputation.

Actions required. Sherman should have anticipated and addressed potential problems with Glenarm by informing them during the employment discussions of his obligation to comply with the AIMR Code and Standards. To make certain that his commitment to ethical behavior and professional conduct fit the philosophy of Glenarm, Sherman should have thoroughly explored the firm's policies regarding personal trading, performance presentation policies, procedures for allocation of trades, disclosure of conflict of interests, supervisors' roles, and other investment management issues addressed by the Code and Standards. The interest of the Glenarm partners in employing a CFA charterholder may or may not indicate a sincere repentance from the firm's shady past, but Sherman should have been aware that future ethical infractions by Glenarm expose Sherman to the risk of violating the Code and Standards. If the Glenarm partners played down their commitment to ethics or were unwilling to discuss those issues with him, Sherman should have recognized a possible signal that he should decline the invitation to join their firm and should have investigated the reasons for their reluctance.

Once at Glenarm, Sherman should present his immediate supervisor with a statement of his obligation to the AIMR Code and Standards and a copy of the *Standards of Practice Handbook.*

Loyalty to One's Employer. Under Standard III(B), Duty to Employer, members are not to undertake any independent practice that could result in compensation or other benefit in competition with their employer unless they obtain written consent from both the employer and the person or entity for whom they will undertake independent practice. Sherman's solicitation of clients and prospects and his plans to take Pearl property for the benefit of Glenarm are a breach of Standard III(B).

Standard III(B) does not preclude members from seeking alternative employment, but it does obligate a member to protect the interests of the employer by refraining from any conduct that could deprive an employer of profit or the benefits of the member's skills and abilities. An employee is free to make arrangements to leave any employer and go into competitive business—so long as the employee's preparations to leave do not breach the employee's duty of loyalty to the current employer.

In this instance, Sherman had an obligation to act in the best interests of Pearl while he was still an employee of Pearl. He had a duty not to engage in any activities that would be detrimental to Pearl's business until his resignation date became effective. The following activities by Sherman violated this duty of loyalty and, as a result, violated Standard III(B).

▦ *Solicitation of clients and prospects.* Sherman's solicitation of clients on behalf of Glenarm while he was still employed at Pearl is a clear violation of Standard III(B). Attempting to lure clients from Pearl to another investment company undermined Pearl's business, and the fact that such activity was carried out "after hours" or in a social context is irrelevant; the damage to Pearl's business was the same. Even after leaving Pearl, Sherman must abide by any additional legal and contractual obligations between himself and Pearl that would prevent solicitation of clients.

Soliciting *potential* clients of Pearl was also a violation of Standard III(B). When engaging in such activity, Sherman was attempting to interfere with Pearl's business opportunities for his own benefit and the benefit of his future employer. Solicitation of clients and prospects cannot begin until Sherman has left Pearl and begun to work for Glenarm.

Sherman's contact of prospects that Pearl had not pursued because of their size or investment objectives does not constitute a violation of Standard III(B) so long as the contacts were not in competition with Pearl in any way. Sherman could solicit business for his new employer on his own time when that activity did not interfere with his responsibilities at Pearl or take away a business opportunity from Pearl.

▨ *Misappropriation of employer property.* Except with the consent of the employer, departing employees may not take property of the employer. Even material prepared by the departing employee is the property of the employer, and taking that property is a violation of the employee's duty to the employer. Employees must obtain permission to take with them any work or work product prepared in the course of the employee's employment or on behalf of the employer.

In this case, all the material mentioned as taken by Sherman was the property of Pearl. Sample marketing material prepared by Sherman, computer program models for stock selection and asset allocation that he developed, and research material and news articles that he collected are all Pearl's property because Sherman's efforts in creating or gathering these materials were undertaken in the context of his employment with and for the benefit of Pearl. Even the list of rejected research ideas was Pearl's property; those ideas were generated by Sherman for Pearl's consideration and use. The analyst that Pearl hires to replace Sherman might benefit by reviewing the list of ideas considered and rejected by the firm.

Actions required. Sherman should have refrained from solicitation of any of Pearl's clients or prospects until he had left Pearl. Sherman should have obtained Pearl's permission to take copies of any work he prepared on behalf of Pearl in the course of his employment there. Without such permission, Sherman should not have taken any material that could have even remotely been considered Pearl's property.

> *Policy statement for a firm.* "Employees shall not undertake any independent practice that could result in compensation or other benefit in competition with the firm unless they obtain written consent from the firm and the person or entity for whom they undertake independent practice. Departing employees shall not engage in any activities that

would be in conflict with this policy, including soliciting firm clients or prospects, removing firm property, or misuse of confidential information."

Disclosure of Additional Compensation and Conflicts. Under Standard III(D), Disclosure of Additional Compensation Arrangements, AIMR members, CFA charterholders, and CFA candidates must disclose to their employers in writing any monetary compensation or other benefits they receive in addition to compensation or benefits conferred by the employer. Because such arrangements may affect an employee's loyalties and objectivity and may create conflicts of interest, employers must receive notice of these arrangements so that they can evaluate employees' actions and motivations.

In the case, Sherman disclosed his consulting arrangements to Pearl but not to Glenarm. Thus, he was violating Standard III(D). Although Sherman's consulting activities might have uncovered investment opportunities for Glenarm clients, the arrangements had the potential to affect Sherman's ability to render objective advice and to divert Sherman's energies away from managing Glenarm clients' portfolios. Sherman should have given Glenarm written information on his independent practice so that the firm could make an informed determination about whether the outside activities impaired his ability to perform his responsibilities with the firm.

Sherman's consulting arrangements are also a violation of Standard III(C), Disclosure of Conflicts to Employer, and Standard IV(A.3), Independence and Objectivity. Under Standard III(C), Sherman has the obligation to disclose all matters that reasonably could be expected to interfere with his duty to Glenarm or ability to make unbiased and objective recommendations. Sherman could wind up receiving consulting fees from the same companies about which he is writing research reports for Glenarm's internal use. Thus, the consulting could compromise Sherman's independence and objectivity and would violate Standard IV(A.3).

Actions required. Sherman must disclose to Glenarm all outside compensation arrangements and describe in detail the activities that gave rise to this compensation. He must obtain written permission in advance of entering into these relationships.

Policy statement for a firm. "Employees shall disclose to the firm in writing all monetary compensation or other benefits that they receive for their services that are in addition to compensation or benefits conferred by the firm. Employees shall also disclose all matters that reasonably could be expected to interfere with their duty to this firm or ability to make unbiased and objective recommendations."

Tore & Associates

Case Facts

Josh Waah is contemplating his first big assignment at Tore & Associates. Waah joined Tore & Associates as an analyst/portfolio assistant one week ago following his graduation from the University of Chicago. His first few days on the job were spent becoming familiar with the firm's investment decision-making methodology, reviewing the four accounts he would be working with, sitting in on an investment strategy meeting, and reading the firm's brief compliance manual. This morning, June 17, 1996, he received his first big project from John Tore, CFA, the founding partner of the firm, and he is deliberating his response.

The Firm. Tore & Associates was formed in January 1994 by John Tore and five former co-workers. All six had previously served as portfolio managers in the corporate trust division of a large Chicago bank. Each of the associates had at least 12 years of investment experience upon leaving the bank, and all are highly regarded equity investment managers.

Tore, a CFA charterholder with 30 years of investment experience, had several opportunities to move into more senior executive positions at the bank, but his preference was to remain a portfolio manager. Dealing with personnel and administrative issues was not attractive to Tore, so he left to found his own firm.

Tore & Associates operates out of offices in the Chicago suburbs and specializes in small- to medium-capitalization stocks. The firm manages the pension plans of 14 companies, all headquartered in the Chicago area. Growth in accounts has been steady, increasing in concert with the strong relative performance achieved by the firm since its inception. Assets under management total $463 million. The firm, registered as an investment advisor with the U.S. Securities and Exchange Commission, has full discretionary authority in managing its clients' pension plans.

At Tore's suggestion, the firm developed a compliance manual based on the AIMR Code of Ethics and Standards of Professional Conduct. Although the manual covered the key AIMR Standards, it did not provide detail on how to implement the Standards at Tore & Associates. All new employees were given the manual on their first day. Tore himself had not read the manual because he believed that, as a CFA charterholder, he was already familiar with AIMR's Code and Standards.

This case was written by Douglas R. Hughes, CFA.

The Toregram. As Waah was finishing his *Wall Street Journal* this Monday morning, Tore's administrative assistant walked in with an interoffice envelope for Waah from Tore. Handing Waah the envelope, the assistant said, "Well, Josh, you know you've been accepted fully into the firm when Mr. Tore sends you one of his infamous 'Toregrams'—or 'Torpedoes' as some of our people call them. If this one involves anything like his other special projects, expect to be derailed from your regular duties for several days—or more. Well, good luck! At least you can take comfort that he has confidence in your abilities."

Waah opened the envelope and read **Exhibit 1**.

What activities discussed in John Tore's memo are in violation of the Code and Standards? Discuss the violations, state what actions Waah should recommend to Tore and his firm to correct the violations, and create short policy statements a firm could use to prevent the violations in the future.

Exhibit 1. Toregram Sent to Waah

Tore & Associates

From the Desk of **John Tore**

To: Josh Waah
Date: June 17, 1996
Subject: Fiduciary Duties

Josh, as you know, our firm prides itself on having considerable expertise in managing equity portfolios. We are being paid (quite handsomely, I might add) to manage the assets of hundreds of people, all of whom depend on us for their present or future livelihood. Needless to say, we take our roles very seriously.

Last week, I read an article about fiduciary obligations that blew my socks off. Specifically, it dealt with the complexities of fiduciary law as well as the stepped-up efforts by the U.S. Department of Labor in enforcing ERISA. As I read the article, I realized how much I didn't know. I thought I had a clear view of my obligations as a fiduciary, but now I'm not so sure. Call me old-fashioned, but I didn't like the sound of words like "breach of duty," "profit disgorgement," "fund restitution," and "personal liability."

My view on fiduciary duties is what it's always been: As fiduciaries, we have the job of preserving and enhancing the financial position of the plan participants and beneficiaries of the clients we serve. We're dealing with funds that ultimately belong to others; these people have put their trust in us, and we must not do anything that would jeopardize that trust.

Our client communication is good, we have honest and admirable intentions, our fees are in line with industry standards, and our performance has been well above average. We try to run a tight ship here while still allowing for some informality (because of my long-held belief that investment ideas and investment decisions are best hatched and nurtured in a relaxed and collegial atmosphere). At the same time, I'm thinking that maybe we need to raise our level of consciousness on fiduciary duties, assess where we are, and formalize our policies and procedures.

As you get to know all of us better, you'll see we embrace a strong sense of duty and professionalism. Our intentions are good, and maybe our activities are also. Do I see any egregious or patently offensive conduct within the firm? No, in fact, I see absolutely no evidence of our people abusing plan assets for their own personal gain, and I'm not aware of any conflicts of interest we have as a firm or as individuals that would affect our actions on behalf of our clients and the plan beneficiaries. Our firm has no corporate ties to our clients that would intrude on the investment process. BUT we may be falling down somewhat through lack of knowledge or lack of proper emphasis.

I may need to be more vigilant than I have been. My past work experience was with a large financial institution that had layers and layers of bureaucracy, gobs of administrative personnel, and a sizable compliance staff, and they handled the legal and regulatory matters. We portfolio managers directed our full efforts to earning the highest returns possible on our portfolios.

None of us here at Tore & Associates are lawyers or have compliance backgrounds. We don't have the education or experience to untangle and interpret the many complexities surrounding fiduciary conduct. What we need are some straightforward, comprehensive comments that will serve as a basis to guide us in our day-to-day investment decisions.

Three areas addressed in the article concern me:

1. Soft Dollars. Like all investment advisory firms, we have brokers competing for our commission business, and we have soft-dollar arrangements in place, although they are not based on anything very elaborate. Every few months, our portfolio managers informally get together with our trader and indicate which brokers have been providing the best research and the most responsive service. We make our decisions on brokerage allocation and soft-dollar purchases on this basis and steer our trading business accordingly.

    In some cases, our trader simply uses his own discretion and goes with the best execution. The clients may not be aware of it, but they are often getting the benefit of low-cost trades. When we do pay up, it's usually in conjunction with something a broker is doing or providing for us. For example, on occasion our portfolio managers may attend broker-sponsored seminars using soft-dollar arrangements, and one broker provides us with the latest in spreadsheet and word-processing software. For the most part, however, the soft dollars represent pure payback for research.

2. Proxy Voting. Our proxy-voting policy is quite simple: Routine proxies are discarded. I don't believe we are really serving our clients by taking the time to ratify a corporate auditor or by voting for an uncontested slate of directors. For more complex proxies, the portfolio managers make decisions on proxy matters for their own accounts. I realize we have a responsibility here, so we generally do vote on controversial issues or those that have particular investment significance. But realistically, if we don't like the corporate direction, we simply sell the stock. It doesn't get much simpler than that. And from a practical standpoint, I ask myself: Does voting proxies bring in new business? No. Do we receive additional fees by voting? No. Is the proxy analysis and voting process time-consuming and expensive? Yes. Can voting the proxy of a sponsor client jeopardize the relationship? You bet! By making a more concerted effort to vote proxies, would our already limited and overworked staff be forced to divert attention away from the primary job at hand (namely, managing portfolios)? Yes, to some extent. Can Tore & Associates really make that much of a difference in a proxy vote? Probably not in most cases. Should we be doing more in dealing with proxies? You tell me.

3. Diversification. Based on our performance history, I believe our portfolio managers adequately diversify their portfolios. I can think of only one case this year when one of our investments went really bad and was responsible for horrible performance for that fund (a product liability suit sank one of our medical technology stocks).

    Some of our clients have placed specific restrictions or stipulations on investment strategy, however, and I'm wondering how we should deal with those situations. For example, two of our clients have instructed us, as spelled out in the plan documents, to invest within very narrow industry sectors (in one instance, computer software companies, and in the other, medium-size regional banks). Confining our investments in these areas has resulted in outstanding performance for the two funds; in fact, we've hit a number of home runs. It's hard to argue with success (talk about benefiting the plan beneficiaries!), but I wonder if a potential problem is looming here. What is our fiduciary duty to our clients that make portfolio restrictions?

Our pension business continues to grow, governmental scrutiny is increasing, and plan participants are more and more aware of their rights in the management of their funds. I think we need to renew our acquaintance with fiduciary duties—and soon!

In short, Josh, I want to know what constitutes fiduciary duty and how well our firm is carrying out its fiduciary duty. And I'd like you to recommend any changes to our compliance manual that you think are appropriate.

I'd like your comments by next Monday.

Case Discussion

This case illustrates how compliance issues can be overlooked in a small firm where portfolio management is the focus of the senior managers' time and interest. John Tore is correct in his view that the primary responsibility of a fiduciary is "to preserve and enhance the financial position of plan participants and beneficiaries." The interests of the plan beneficiaries must come ahead of the interests of the plan sponsor, Tore & Associates, and the individual portfolio manager. Tore's candid appraisals of how the firm deals with soft dollars, proxies, and portfolio diversification indicate, however, that the interests of plan beneficiaries do not always receive priority. Breaches of fiduciary duty are clearly in evidence at the firm.

General Fiduciary Duties. Standard IV(B.1), Fiduciary Duties, states, "In relationships with clients, members shall use particular care in determining applicable fiduciary duty and shall comply with such duty as to those persons and interests to whom the duty is owed." Tore and his associates need to understand that through their investment management relationships, they owe the plan beneficiaries and their pension clients a duty of loyalty that supersedes all other interests.

As a CFA charterholder, Tore is also obligated, under Standard I, Fundamental Responsibilities, to be knowledgeable about and comply with applicable laws and regulations relating to fiduciary duty. By virtue of its U.S. domicile and investment discretion over the management of private pension funds, Tore & Associates serves in a fiduciary capacity and is subject to the fiduciary rules and standards set forth by the Employee Retirement Income Security Act. Tore thus has a responsibility to comply with ERISA rules and regulations.

Under ERISA, a fiduciary must

- act solely in the interest of the plan participants and beneficiaries and for the exclusive purpose of benefiting the plan's participants and beneficiaries,
- act with the care, skill, prudence, and diligence of a prudent person acting in like capacity,
- diversify the plan's investments in order to protect it from the risk of substantial loss,
- act in accordance with the provisions of the plan documents to the extent that they comply with ERISA, and
- refrain from engaging in prohibited transactions as defined by ERISA.

Actions required. Waah needs to impress on Tore that the firm, serving in a fiduciary capacity, owes absolute loyalty to the plan beneficiaries. He and his associates must avoid placing themselves in situations where they have interests that conflict with those of the underlying owners of the plan assets.

Policy statement for a firm. "Preeminent among our fiduciary obligations is the duty to act solely in the interest of plan participants and beneficiaries, with an overriding goal of preserving the assets and optimizing their value. In addition, all employees are required to adhere to the basic rules of loyalty, prudence, and diversification."

Soft Dollars. As discussed in the explanation of Standard IV(B.1) in the *Standards of Practice Handbook*, to comply with U.S. fiduciary and securities laws, investment managers should use the following guidelines with regard to the use of soft dollars.

First, investment managers should use soft dollars for the exclusive benefit of portfolio beneficiaries. Tore & Associates (as distinct from its clients and plan beneficiaries) should receive no benefit other than the agreed-upon compensation arrangements with brokers, and the firm should not seek to further its own interests through the use of plan assets (brokerage commissions are considered plan assets). Tore admitted that certain general office expenses were paid for by a broker through soft-dollar arrangements, which is a clear breach of fiduciary duty; depending on their nature and the extent of expenses incurred, broker-sponsored seminars could be considered a violation as well. An argument could be made that the "excess commissions" paid were wrongfully appropriated client assets diverted to Tore & Associates' own benefit.

Second, investment managers should pay commissions that are reasonable in relation to the services received. Tore does not have a formal set of procedures for selecting brokers with whom soft-dollar arrangements are established or for evaluating the value of research and other services used in the firm's investment decision making. Tore needs to establish and follow a sound formal process for analyzing brokerage arrangements and transaction costs to ensure that client assets are not wrongfully appropriated for the benefit of the fiduciary.

A 1975 amendment to the Securities Exchange Act provides a "safe harbor" for investment managers using soft-dollar arrangements. Section 28(e) states that an investment manager has not breached his or her fiduciary duty by paying a commission in excess of best-execution price "if such commission was reasonable in relation to the value of the brokerage and research services provided." In a 1986 Interpretive Release, the SEC clarified and revised the standard in 28(e) with respect to the definition of brokerage and research services: Research is defined as "essentially that which provides assistance to the money manager in the performance of his investment decision-making responsibilities." Accordingly, Tore & Associates *is* allowed to "pay up" in brokerage commissions if the amount of a commission is reasonable in relation to the value of the brokerage and research services received (the firm itself is allowed to make this determination, under the assumption that the determination will be made in good faith).

To establish that commissions are reasonable, Tore also needs to maintain adequate records of soft-dollar transactions. The memo states, "We have soft-dollar arrangements in place, although they are not based on anything very elaborate" and "our portfolio managers informally get together with our trader." The language implies that Tore & Associates keeps no records pertaining to brokerage allocation and its practices in this area. The firm would thus have no basis for defending itself if its selection/allocation procedures were brought into question by a regulator or court of law.

Third, investment managers should disclose soft-dollar arrangements to clients. Tore's comment that "clients may not be aware of it" is a strong indication that communication with clients is limited or nonexistent with respect to soft-dollar arrangements and brokerage allocations.

Above all, Tore & Associates has an obligation always to seek the best price and execution on its trades, the benefits of which will accrue directly to plan beneficiaries and its clients.

Actions required. Tore & Associates needs to ensure that the services received from brokers have decision-making value commensurate with their cost. The firm needs to evaluate the full range and quality of brokers' services—execution capability, quality of research, and broker responsiveness. In addition, the firm should take into account such factors as commission rate (and its component parts). The firm needs a formal process for evaluating and deciding soft-dollar arrangements and needs to maintain written records of its soft-dollar practices. Soft-dollar arrangements must be disclosed to clients.

> *Policy statements for a firm.* "Employees and the firm as a whole are forbidden from using brokerage commissions or any other client (or the plan participants' and beneficiaries') assets for their own benefit. The firm shall keep accurate and detailed records reflecting transactions involving soft dollars, and disclose soft-dollar practices to clients."

> **Proxy Policy.** Proxy-voting rights are considered assets of a pension plan; therefore, proxy voting involves the exercise of fiduciary responsibility. Because Tore & Associates has discretionary authority to manage fund assets, the firm has the duty to vote proxies associated with those assets. The memo reflects that Tore is not taking his responsibilities seriously. As a plan fiduciary, Tore & Associates cannot be a passive shareholder. The firm must

cast its votes in a way that will maximize the economic value of plan holdings. Failing to vote or casting a vote without considering its impact may violate the firm's duty of loyalty to its clients under Standard IV(B.1).

Tore's memo indicates that routine proxies are not voted, that the portfolio managers have authority in some issues, and that little thought is being given to consistency in proxy-voting policy or a thorough examination of the underlying proxy issues. Specific guidelines and a regular review process appear to be lacking at the firm. Apparently, record keeping is minimal or nonexistent. Adequate record keeping would include keeping a record of stock held, reconciling proxies received with stock held, tracing missing proxies, and keeping a record of how and why proxies were voted.

Actions required. Tore & Associates must vote proxies in an informed and responsible manner. The firm must independently examine the underlying issues on a case-by-case basis. To ensure proper proxy procedures are carried out, the firm should prepare a written description of the steps it follows, train employees in the procedures, and designate someone to monitor the process. If routine proxy issues are to be handled differently from more controversial ones, the firm needs to establish a definition of "routine" and "nonroutine." Tore should establish a review process for unusual or controversial proposals. Major proxy issues should be identified by particular accounts, and the preferences of beneficiaries and participants should be noted.

> *Policy statement for a firm.* "In all proxy situations, the firm, as the investment manager, has a duty to make independent proxy decisions and to decide with objectivity what is in the best interests of the beneficiaries for whom a proxy is voted. All proxies should be voted."

Diversification. As a fiduciary for corporate pension plans, Tore & Associates has a duty under ERISA, as noted in the discussion of Standard IV(B.1) in the *Handbook*, to "diversify the plan's investments to protect it from the risk of substantial loss." Although plan documents are the primary determinants of a fiduciary's duty, conformance with the applicable law— in this case, ERISA—is mandatory. Therefore, notwithstanding the plan document directives or subsequent investment performance, Tore & Associates has failed to invest prudently by limiting all the assets of one plan to computer software companies and all the assets of another plan to medium-size regional banks.

Actions required. Tore & Associates should develop guidelines for prudent diversification of portfolios. Prior to the inclusion of a new account, Tore & Associates must judge the appropriateness of the objectives set forth in the plan documents for the specific plan. Tore & Associates should also investigate whether the plan directives are permissible under applicable law; if not, they should be brought into conformance or Tore & Associates should refuse to accept the account. The associates need to revise the plan documents pertaining to the two existing concentrated portfolios to allow for broader diversification. If the plan sponsors refuse, Tore should resign from the account.

> *Policy statements for a firm.* "The firm will diversify investments of the plans under its control so as to minimize the risk of loss."
>
> "Plan documents are to be followed only to the extent they are consistent with the firm's requirements and applicable fiduciary and securities rules and regulations."

Process versus Performance. Tore & Associates appears to have no liability for the investment that lost its entire value as a result of a product liability lawsuit so long as Tore & Associates had a reasonable and well-defined investment decision-making process in place at the time of purchase and this process was followed. A loss (even a total loss) on an investment would not be considered imprudent per se. ERISA's Prudent Expert Rule requires a pension plan fiduciary to exercise the care, skill, and diligence under the circumstances then prevailing that a prudent person acting in like capacity and familiar with such matters would use in the conduct of an enterprise of a like character and with like aims. As reflected in the *Handbook* discussion of Standard IV(B.1), the duty to act as a prudent expert is satisfied with respect to a particular investment if the fiduciary has thoroughly considered the investment's place in the whole portfolio, the risk of loss and opportunity for gains as well as the diversification, liquidity, cash flow, and overall return requirements of the pension plan or the portion of the pension plan assets for which the manager is responsible.

The key question for investment recommendations and actions is: Does this particular course of action further the plan's purposes?

Two other Standards of Professional Conduct are applicable to the issue of prudence, rationality, and structure in the firm's investment decision-making process. Standard IV(A.1), Reasonable Basis and Representations, requires an investment manager to "exercise diligence and thoroughness in making investment recommendations or in taking investment actions" and to "have a reasonable and adequate basis . . . for such recommendations or actions." Standard IV(B.2), Portfolio Investment Recommendations and Actions, requires an investment manager to "make a reasonable inquiry into a client's financial situation, investment experience, and investment objectives prior to making any investment recommendations," "update this information as necessary," and "consider the appropriateness and suitability of investment recommendations or actions for each portfolio or client."

U.S. courts have based findings of imprudence less on the specific investment at issue than on the fiduciary's (1) failure to undertake a thorough and diligent analysis of the merits of an investment that may have been unsuitable or (2) failure to consider alternative investments that offered more favorable risk–return trade-offs. The emphasis is on competence and process rather than results of the investment decision.

Actions required. Tore & Associates must ensure that its investment decision-making process is built around a well-reasoned analysis of the merits and suitability of investment. Once an investment has been added to the portfolio, Tore & Associates must continue to monitor the investment, the portfolio, and the market in case changing circumstances necessitate portfolio adjustments.

> *Policy statement for a firm.* "Firm employees will make investment decisions only after exercising thoroughness and diligence and ensuring that the investments are suitable for the particular fund involved."

Moosehead Investment Management

Case Facts

Colin Allenson, CFA, chief investment officer of Moosehead Investment Management, is sitting in his office holding a formal "Notice of Inquiry" from AIMR's Professional Conduct Program (PCP). The notice states that both he and the president and chief executive officer of Moosehead, Ronald Vincent, CFA, are under investigation for violating Standard V(B), Performance Presentation, and Standard III(E), Responsibilities of Supervisors. As a CFA charterholder, Allenson knows that he and Vincent must cooperate fully with the PCP's investigation, even if it leads to a professional conduct hearing and disciplinary sanctions; otherwise, they risk losing their CFA designations for failure to cooperate in an investigation. Allenson is shocked that his professional conduct has been challenged and is reviewing the chain of events leading to this predicament.

Moosehead History. Moosehead Investment Management is a medium-sized company that provides investment management service for retirement plans, endowment funds, corporations, individuals, and trusts. Vincent and Allenson, who also serves as compliance officer, founded the company in 1986 with approximately $30 million under management. By 1991, the company had reached a high of $750 million under management. During the next two years, however, as a result of mediocre returns, the company lost several clients and slipped to $500 million.

In order to regain assets and restore Moosehead to its former position, Vincent and Allenson decided to seek a high-profile portfolio manager with a strong marketing background who could boost the firm's returns and actively recruit new investment clients.

In 1993, after a lengthy search, Vincent and Allenson agreed to hire Maggie Cassidy, chair and CEO of Katadan Asset Management, a small investment management firm with approximately $150 million under management. Cassidy had started Katadan in 1983 and slowly built the company by combining excellent returns and aggressive marketing tactics. Cassidy's marketing background and uncanny ability to post excellent returns consistently, even during bear markets, impressed Vincent and Allenson.

This case was written by Jonathan Stokes, Esq., AIMR.

Prior to Cassidy's arrival, Allenson was responsible for calculating performance and preparing the marketing presentations used by Moosehead to attract new clients. As part of Moosehead's restructuring, these responsibilities were delegated to Cassidy. Although Allenson has direct supervisory authority to control Cassidy's actions, Vincent has the ultimate authority to discipline Cassidy, including the power to fire the new manager.

For the first three years after Cassidy's arrival, Moosehead reported markedly improved performance. Cassidy took full advantage of this improvement in her presentations and marketing materials to clients and prospects. In addition, following an industry trend, Cassidy declared in Moosehead's performance presentation information that the firm complies with AIMR's Performance Presentation Standards (PPS). As a result, Moosehead's assets under management now top $1 billion. All three managers are making more money than they ever have, and Vincent and Allenson are very happy they hired Cassidy.

Performance Presentations. Early in 1996, Cassidy and Allenson made a presentation to the trustees of the Our Sisters of Mercy Hospital Employee Retirement Plan in an effort to make Moosehead the investment manager for the $50 million fund. The sisters, not being very sophisticated in such secular subjects as investment management, retained Powell Williams, CFA, as a consultant to help them choose an investment manager for the fund.

Prior to the presentation, Cassidy sent an investment management proposal to Williams that included a page called "Capital Appreciation Accounts" (see **Figure 1**). Williams reviewed the material thoroughly and discovered the following footnote:

Rates of return are calculated in accordance with AIMR standards. From 1983 to 1986, returns are in accordance with AIMR's Performance Presentation Standards except that they are not size weighted. The composite includes accounts managed that were fully discretionary and more than $250,000 in value, gross of management fees, custody fees, and commission charges. Results from 1986 to 1993 are from a model portfolio. Performance data are historical and should not be interpreted as an indicator of future results.

Williams, in his position as consultant for pension funds seeking asset managers, is very familiar with AIMR's PPS and, after Cassidy and Allenson made their presentation, pointed out several discrepancies between the material and the PPS, including the fact that although Moosehead has been in existence since only 1986, the performance sheet listed performance results from 1983.

Allenson, who had no involvement in the preparation of the proposal

Figure 1. Moosehead Capital Appreciation Accounts

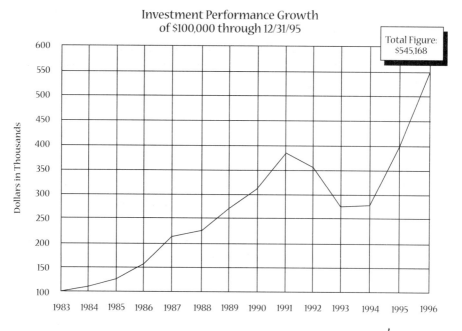

Moosehead Investment Management, Inc.
Capital Appreciation Accounts

Investment Performance Growth
of $100,000 through 12/31/95

Total Figure:
$545,168

Dollars in Thousands

**Moosehead Investment
Management, Inc.
Annual Returns
For Capital Appreciation Accounts:**

1983	+11.0%
1984	+16.0%
1985	+21.0%
1986	+41.2%
1987	+3.2%
1988	+19.5%
1989	+12.9%
1990	+26.7%
1991	-8.6%
1992	-23.9%
1993	+1.3%
1994	+45.0%
1995	+37.5%

→ firm started in 86

Note: Rates of return are calculated in accordance with AIMR standards. ✗ From 1983 to 1986, returns are in accordance with AIMR's Performance Presentation Standards except that they are not size weighted. The composite includes accounts managed ✗ that were fully discretionary and more than $250,000 in value, *gross of* management fees, custody fees, ✗ and commission charges. Results from 1986 to 1993 are from a model portfolio. ✗ Performance data are historical and should not be interpreted as an indicator of future results.

material and little familiarity with the PPS, deferred to Cassidy. Cassidy, looking a little sheepish, muttered something about "technicalities" and stated that the presentation met "the spirit" of the PPS. She admitted that she adopted Katadan Asset Management's performance numbers for the years 1983 through 1986 as the performance of Moosehead.

After the meeting, Williams wrote a letter to Allenson and Cassidy thanking them for their interest but explaining that the sisters were afraid of investing with a "fly-by-night operation" and did not want to invest their money with any company with fewer then 12 years of experience. Williams also expressed surprise that Allenson and Vincent, two CFA charterholders, were claiming compliance with the PPS but were not familiar with the basic PPS requirements. He suggested that the two become more familiar with the PPS and revise their presentation materials if Moosehead planned to continue to claim compliance.

Although Cassidy seemed to shrug off Williams's upbraiding, Allenson was thoroughly embarrassed. He asked Cassidy if all the firm's presentation materials contained similarly egregious errors. Cassidy assured him that the presentation to the Sisters of Mercy was an isolated matter and that all the other marketing materials met the requirements of the PPS to the letter. Cassidy also assured Allenson that she would thoroughly review all future reports personally to ensure that they met the requirements.

Allenson was skeptical of Cassidy's claims but relied on her assurances and did not pursue the matter. Allenson took no steps to familiarize himself with the AIMR PPS and did not report the incident to Vincent.

One month later, Allenson and Cassidy made a similar presentation to another potential client. During the presentation, Allenson noticed that this proposal contained exactly the same performance presentation material used in the meeting with Williams. Although the potential client said nothing about the performance material and eventually hired Moosehead as investment manager, Allenson was furious.

Moosehead had no formal compliance procedures, and rather than confronting Cassidy, Allenson decided to conduct an investigation of Cassidy's performance calculations and marketing practices. He found that since Cassidy had been given responsibility for performance calculation and reporting, she had

- reported Katadan's performance figures from 1983 through 1986 as Moosehead's without disclosing the source of the figures;
- derived performance figures for certain categories of accounts by using hypothetical, rather than actual, data in the form of component weightings, without disclosing this fact to investors; and
- based the reported performance figures for the firm's composites on a select group of accounts, which varied from quarter to quarter.

Allenson determined that Cassidy's practices resulted in the firm repeatedly advertising to current and potential clients significantly better performance than the composites actually attained.

Allenson reported his findings to Vincent with a recommendation that the firm immediately terminate Cassidy's employment and distribute the correct performance information to all clients and potential clients.

Vincent acknowledged the violations but wanted to confront Cassidy with the findings and get her side of the story. Business had been going well, largely as a result of Cassidy's efforts, and Vincent told Allenson he did not want to "rock the boat" by putting too much pressure on Cassidy. Vincent also expressed reluctance to report the revised performance numbers to clients because he feared they would withdraw their accounts.

When confronted by Vincent, Cassidy repeated the assurances made to Allenson that the problems were isolated and would never happen again. Vincent accepted these promises and continued to give Cassidy wide discretion in creating Moosehead's performance reports. He assumed that Allenson would keep him informed of any further misconduct by Cassidy.

Cassidy and Allenson continued to hand out performance information that claimed compliance with the PPS in their presentations to potential clients. Allenson assumed, because he had reported his findings to Vincent and recommended that Cassidy be fired, that Cassidy's conduct was no longer his responsibility and that Vincent would eventually address the matter. Although he was present during the client presentations made by Cassidy with the erroneous material and recognized that the material was still grossly misleading, Allenson said nothing.

When Cassidy forwarded an investment management proposal to the Piscataquis County Employees Retirement Fund, the fund manager forwarded the material to the county's investment consultant—Powell Williams. Once again, Williams immediately recognized the egregious discrepancies between the material and the PPS, and he was astonished that Moosehead continued to claim compliance with the PPS. This time, he forwarded both of the Moosehead proposals, together with his previous letter to Allenson and Cassidy, to AIMR's Professional Conduct Program and the U.S. Securities and Exchange Commission.

> *Identify the activities that violated AIMR's Code of Ethics and Standards of Professional Conduct. State what Vincent and Allenson should have done or should do to correct the violations, and draft a short policy statement that a firm might use to prevent such violations.*

Case Discussion

In an effort to expand their business, Donald Vincent and Colin Allenson hired a staff member who violated Standard V(B), Performance Presentation. Their failure to correct her violations has led to their own violations of Standard V(B) and Standard III(E), Responsibilities of Supervisors.

Misrepresentation of Performance. Standard V(B) states that "members shall not make any statements, orally or in writing, that misrepresent the investment performance that they or their firm have accomplished . . . ." This provision requires AIMR members to make every reasonable effort to ensure that performance is communicated to clients or prospects in a fair, accurate, and complete presentation.

In this instance, the information communicated by Moosehead to clients and prospects contained false and material misrepresentations of performance. Moosehead advertised the purported performance numbers of Katadan Asset Management as the performance of Moosehead without disclosing this fact. This practice implied that Moosehead had a longer history of good performance than it actually did. Moosehead also failed to disclose that the advertised performance was not the performance of the entire composite of similar accounts in the firm but only selected accounts. Because the selected accounts differed from quarter to quarter, the presentation presented no meaningful numbers by which to compare performance for either Moosehead itself from year to year or with other companies. All these practices were intentionally adopted to enhance the track record of Moosehead's investments for the express purpose of attracting clients to the firm.

Maggie Cassidy, as the author of the performance presentation reports, clearly violated Standard V(B) by disseminating false and materially misleading information. Allenson and Vincent, by acquiescing in the false and misleading statements, are just as guilty of violating Standard V(B) as if they had drafted the reports themselves. Allenson allowed Cassidy to use the material even after he knew the information it contained was false and misleading. As a result, Allenson and Vincent violated Standard I, Fundamental Responsibilities, by assisting in violations of the Code and Standards and SEC antifraud regulations.

False Claim of Compliance with the PPS. Moosehead's marketing material also claimed compliance with the Performance Presentation Standards. The PPS are intended to promote full disclosure and fair representation in the reporting of investment results. Although members are not required to comply with the PPS, to make a false claim of compliance with the PPS without meeting their requirements is a violation of Standard V(B).

The performance sheet presented by Moosehead shown in Figure 1 violated the PPS in several ways:
- Performance may not be presented as being "in compliance except for," because to claim compliance with the PPS, firms must carry out *all* the mandatory disclosures and meet any other requirements or make any other disclosures necessary to that firm's specific situation.
- Commission charges must be included in performance returns.

- Firm composites must include only actual assets under management; model results may be presented only as supplementary information— and only when the model results are identified as such. Model results may not be linked to actual results.
- The presentation sheet does not show the number of portfolios, the composite assets, or composites as a percentage of firm assets. In addition, the performance sheet does not state that a list of composites is available.

By claiming compliance without being in compliance, Vincent and Allenson are violating not only the PPS but also Standard V(B), because they are misleading clients and prospects about the firm's past performance.

Responsibilities of Supervisors. AIMR members with supervisory responsibility must exercise reasonable supervision over those subject to their authority to prevent violations of applicable statutes and regulations or provisions of AIMR's Code and Standards. In this case, Vincent, who has overall supervisory responsibilities for the firm, and Allenson, who has direct supervisory responsibility for performance presentation and is the compliance officer, can be sanctioned for violating Standard III(E).

    Direct supervisor. Even when Allenson was unaware that Cassidy was engaging in gross misconduct, he had responsibility for Cassidy's actions. Allenson failed to perform an adequate review of the material developed by Cassidy and neglected to implement procedures to monitor Cassidy's activities.

Not only did Allenson fail to exercise his authority at the outset of the relationship, he shirked his supervisory responsibility even after he initially became aware of Cassidy's misconduct. Once the consultant, Powell Williams, pointed out Cassidy's violations of the PPS, Allenson had a duty to determine whether other instances of unreported misconduct had occurred. He also should have reported the matter to Vincent immediately, because Cassidy's actions directly affected fundamental aspects of firm business. Instead, Allenson failed to respond to apparent indications of wrongdoing and improperly relied on the assurances of Cassidy that the problem was an isolated incident. After the disclosure of the misconduct, Cassidy continued to falsify performance presentation to attract clients. Had Allenson placed limits on Cassidy's activities after discovering the misconduct, the firm could have prevented further violations of the law and the Code and Standards.

When Allenson finally, albeit belatedly, conducted an investigation of Cassidy's misconduct and reported the pattern of abuses to Vincent with a recommendation that Cassidy's employment be terminated, his supervisory responsibility did not end. Allenson continued to bear direct responsibility for Cassidy even after he had reported the matter to more senior executives in the firm. Unless he was relieved of his responsibilities as Cassidy's direct supervisor, Allenson had a duty to continue appropriate supervisory action. When Cassidy continued to engage in misconduct, Allenson improperly ignored the behavior and shirked his supervisory role by assuming that a superior in the firm would address the problem.

When Allenson realized that Vincent was doing nothing to prevent Cassidy's wrongdoing, Allenson should have told Vincent that he no longer would be responsible for Cassidy's conduct and, at a minimum, should have refused to participate in client development efforts. If an AIMR member cannot discharge supervisory responsibilities because of the absence, or inadequacy, of a compliance system or the refusal of senior managers to adopt compliance procedures or punish misconduct, the member should decline to accept supervisory responsibility until the firm adopts reasonable procedures that allow adequate supervision.

■ *Overall supervisor.* As president and CEO of the company, Vincent has the ultimate responsibility for the actions of all employees at Moosehead. Senior managers often, however, cannot personally evaluate the conduct of all their employees on a continuing basis. They exercise their authority by delegating supervisory responsibility and establishing and implementing procedures designed to detect and prevent violations. Those with responsibility are expected to know what constitutes an adequate compliance system for the firm, and once the compliance procedures are established, they must also make reasonable efforts to ensure the procedures are enforced.

Vincent delegated to Allenson the responsibility of supervising Cassidy, but delegation of supervisory responsibilities does not relieve Vincent of duties under the Code and Standards. Vincent did not ensure that procedures existed to allow Allenson to supervise Cassidy properly by verifying that the performance numbers and the claims of compliance with AIMR's PPS were valid. Appropriate procedures would have included periodic independent review of the performance records by the compliance department, verification by an independent third party, and a requirement that any serious problem of employee misconduct be reported to Vincent. Because no compliance procedures existed, Vincent failed in his responsibility as supervisor.

In medium or large organizations, those in authority must exercise particular vigilance when they are made aware of irregularities. Once Allenson made Vincent aware of Cassidy's violations of the law and the Code and Standards, Vincent had a responsibility to respond vigorously. Although he did not have to monitor the situation personally, he at least had to initiate an investigation to determine what had occurred and whether other instances of misconduct had gone unreported. Pending the outcome of the investigation, Vincent should have required increased supervision of Cassidy. Instead, Vincent improperly relied on the assurances of Cassidy and failed, or refused, to take any action.

Vincent's inadequate response apparently was influenced by the important role Cassidy had played in the success of the firm. Cassidy was a "big producer" who, despite blatant wrongdoing, was allowed to continue her abuses in order to benefit the firm to the detriment of investors. AIMR members must not allow business considerations to interfere with their duty to adhere to high ethical and professional standards.

Defining responsibilities among multiple supervisors. If more than one supervisor is involved, the roles of each must be clearly defined. In this case, both Vincent and Allenson apparently believed that someone else would take the supervisory action necessary to respond to Cassidy's conduct. Allenson believed that mere reporting of the matter to Vincent relieved him of supervisory responsibility. Vincent assumed that Allenson would continue to monitor Cassidy and report further misconduct. Although Allenson recommended terminating Cassidy, Vincent and Allenson did not discuss what action would be taken or who would be responsible for taking action.

When supervisors are aware of wrongdoing, they have a duty to define the responsibilities of those who are to respond. Because Vincent and Allenson failed in this regard, they both bear some measure of responsibility for the failure to take action.

Policy statement for a firm. "Those in the firm who hold supervisory positions shall implement appropriate policies and procedures that will allow them to adequately monitor the employees under their control. These procedures shall be reviewed by top management on a regular basis, and at least annually, to ensure sufficiency and legality. The scope of each supervisor's responsibility and authority shall be clearly stated and shall remain in effect until explicitly terminated in writing. Supervisors shall disseminate their policies and procedures to appropriate personnel.

"Any professional misconduct shall be reported to top management. Should violations occur, supervisors shall investigate the matter promptly and thoroughly to determine the scope of the wrongdoing. Supervisors shall adopt additional measures to monitor the conduct of an employee under investigation and place appropriate limitations on the employee pending the outcome of the investigation. If more than one employee with supervisory responsibility should become involved in the investigation, the supervisors shall clearly define the responsibility of those who will respond."

International Investment Advisors

Case Facts

Laura Manning, CFA, the president of International Investment Advisors (IIA), a Boston-based international money management firm, is sitting in her firm's Geneva, Switzerland, office trying to sort out several situations that her compliance officer in Geneva has just brought to her attention. The compliance officer, Joseph Wong, met Manning at the airport and, during the ride to the office, brought up several concerns he has about the firm's use of commission soft dollars. Manning flew into Geneva earlier in the day for what was to be a routine visit. Now she is deep in thought about her responsibilities as a CFA charterholder subject to AIMR's Code of Ethics and Standards of Professional Conduct and how her actions will conform or conflict with those guidelines.

Emerging Markets Seminar. Wong's most pressing concern was a request by the firm's marketing department that soft dollars be used to send two marketing people to a seminar on emerging markets investing. The seminar is scheduled to begin in a week, and Wong needs to determine whether to pay for the occasion with soft dollars or hard dollars. The cost of the seminar and of sending several employees to New York City to attend the seminar for three days is fairly large. In the car, Wong made clear to Manning that, although he wants to help keep expenses as low as possible, in his opinion, this use of soft dollars does not fall within the provisions of IIA's soft-dollar policies established in Boston. Wong asked whether all of IIA's U.S. soft-dollar policies, which were established to meet the safe-harbor provisions of Section 28(e) of the U.S. Securities Exchange Act of 1934, are applicable to the Geneva office. To hear both sides of the issue, Manning met with Peter Hauk, the head of marketing in Geneva, to discuss the emerging markets conference. Hauk told Manning that because of all the recent interest in emerging markets, this seminar might be useful for acquiring new clients for the firm. Hauk also indicated that the seminar could help educate the marketing staff about the risks involved in emerging markets investing.

Although IIA is a global firm comprising separate legal entities in each of 10 countries, it has always maintained integrated investment processes;

This case was written by Paul F. Van Schyndel, CFA, State Street Global Advisors.

so, all of its various offices worldwide provide input to the investment decisions of the firm and can share research generated in other offices. IIA uses a team-oriented system of decision making. In this approach, Hauk argued, marketing personnel are an integral part of helping clients determine their investment objectives, constraints, and asset allocations, as well as being responsible for assisting clients with ongoing monitoring of their accounts.

Hauk stated that he does not want this type of expense to come out of his department's budget. He prefers to pay for it with the soft dollars, which are "not real money and are just sitting around waiting to be used." One of the employees Hauk intends to send to the seminar is a Swiss citizen and the other is a U.S. employee on temporary assignment to Geneva from the Boston office marketing staff.

Hauk indicated that Chermante Securities, a Swiss brokerage firm through which the IIA Geneva office executes trades, is willing to cover the seminar bills via commission soft dollars IIA has accumulated in its account with Chermante. These commissions were generated by the trades of a number of clients—Swiss and U.S. (some clients of IIA's Boston office). Hauk also told Manning that Chermante is eager to help out because it only this year became a broker for the Geneva office.

Turbot Fisheries. The second issue that Wong raised with Manning concerned one of the Geneva office's largest U.S. clients, Turbot Fisheries Pension Fund, based in Portland, Maine. The fund's treasurer, Barbara Buckley, recently requested that 30 percent of the fund's trades be directed through a specific broker, Rushmann Securities, so that commission dollars generated from the pension plan's account can be used by Turbot.

Turbot started out as a client in IIA's Boston office and recently requested that a portion of its pension fund be invested internationally in stable, developed countries. Turbot's senior managers liked the prestige of having some of the company's money managed in Switzerland and specifically requested that the pension fund's international exposure be managed by IIA's Geneva office. Wong told Manning that he suspects one of the reasons Geneva was so desirable was that Buckley, who likes to ski, would be able to visit Switzerland several times a year.

Wong informed Manning that Rushmann Securities is not highly regarded by IIA's traders or the local Geneva financial community. Rushmann is known as a broker that provides questionable execution and charges high fees for its services. Wong reported that IIA's traders in Geneva had been quite upset about Turbot's suggestion because they disliked the idea that they would be forced to deal with such a broker. To make matters worse, Wong had heard that Buckley intends to use the commissions recaptured by the pension fund to pay for gifts and exotic vacation trips for Turbot treasury employees Buckley wants to reward for outstanding work performance. Although Wong does not want to ruin this client relationship, he is concerned that this use of commission dollars is an illegal activity.

> *Explain what violations of the Standards have occurred or could occur in this case and indicate a proper course of action for Manning to take in those instances. Provide short policy statements a firm could use to prevent the violations.*

Case Discussion

Specific violations of the Code and Standards have not yet occurred at International Investment Advisors, but if Laura Manning does not take the proper steps, infractions may soon result. Manning must determine which of several regulations to follow in two countries and must respond to a request by the marketing department and requests by a client that may lead IIA into illegalities.

Fundamental Responsibilities. In considering marketing's use of soft dollars, Manning must proceed cautiously in order not to violate Swiss or U.S. law or IIA's own policies. As a CFA charterholder, Manning has the additional responsibility of complying with AIMR's Code and Standards. In this situation, Manning's responsibilities are complicated by the fact that IIA operates in more than one country and that the regulations in each of these countries are unlikely to be consistent.

In examining legal restrictions, Manning's first aim is to determine the requirements of the laws and regulations applicable to this situation. The applicable law must be followed. If the applicable law governing the conduct is less strict than AIMR's Code and Standards in addressing the activity, Manning must follow the Code and Standards. Manning should be systematic and logical in her approach to sorting out this issue and should make sure that she does not violate any of AIMR's requirements—in particular Standard I, Fundamental Responsibilities, which imposes a requirement that she know and comply with all applicable laws governing her professional activities.

Although strong arguments are being made by IIA's marketing department that the emerging markets seminar is an allowable use of soft dollars, to take this stance would be a stretch under current U.S. law. Section 28(e) of the Securities Exchange Act provides a safe harbor for the payment of soft-dollar commissions by an investment manager to a broker for research services—that is, services that assist a manager in the investment decision-making process. The emerging markets seminar might provide legitimate research that could be paid for with soft dollars; whether it is research oriented could be easily determined by a review of the seminar subject matter and presenters. Sending a marketing person to this seminar, however, does not fall within the definition of research services contemplated by Section 28(e) because marketing persons generally are not directly involved in investment decision making. The expense would thus not be an allowable use of soft dollars under U.S. law. In addition, nonresearch aspects of the trip—such as travel, lodging, and meals—do not fall under the safe harbor and would not be allowed under U.S. law.

Manning needs to review IIA's soft-dollar policies and determine whether the policies established for the United States are applied by IIA in all its offices. If IIA has one set of soft-dollar policies that are applied globally, then the Geneva office must comply with IIA restrictions so long as they meet or exceed applicable local law. If IIA lets each foreign site determine its own policies based on local law, then Manning should find out what the restrictions are in the Swiss guidelines and make sure they are being followed.

Assuming that Swiss law is silent on the issue of soft dollars, firms operating in Switzerland can decide individually what kinds of activities will be paid for in this manner. For U.S. clients managed in Geneva, the higher standard on soft dollars is set by U.S. law; therefore, IIA may wish to require all its foreign offices to meet that standard. Another solution that would resolve the conflict with U.S. law would be to separate the commission dollars generated by Swiss clients from those generated by U.S. clients and use those segregated commissions as each country permits.

In either case, Manning also has a responsibility as a supervisor to see that appropriate compliance procedures have been established and communicated to covered personnel at the headquarters and in the firm's foreign offices and that these policies are being monitored and enforced [see the following discussion of Standard III(E), Responsibilities of Supervisors].

Actions required. Manning should start by looking at the requirements and restrictions imposed by law, both U.S. and Swiss; restrictions imposed by IIA's internal policies and procedures; and any responsibilities that she must meet as a CFA charterholder.

> ***Policy statement for a firm.*** "Soft dollars will be used for the payment of research services only. Seminars, conferences, and courses may be paid for in soft dollars if the activity qualifies as bona fide research. Designated supervisory personnel of the firm will review all proposed soft-dollar payments prior to authorizing them."

Committing or Assisting Violations. Chermante Securities has offered to pay for the emerging markets seminar, most likely because the company wants to curry favor with its new client. Manning needs to determine which soft-dollar payments she may legally authorize in order to avoid violating or assisting in a violation of the law.

Actions required. Manning should not authorize Chermante to pay for the seminar until she is confident that the payments are allowed by law. If Manning is unsure of the applicability of this area of law, she should discuss the issue with her compliance officer or with competent legal counsel. Specific requirements for complying with applicable governing laws should be incorporated into IIA's compliance policies. At a minimum, Manning must assure herself that IIA will receive best price and execution from Chermante and that the commission charged is reasonable in relation to the service provided by Chermante to IIA.

> *Policy statement for a firm.* "The payment of commissions to a broker for research services (soft-dollar services) must meet the requirements set forth by applicable governing laws."

Fiduciary Duty. Turbot Fisheries, a major client of IIA, has requested that a specific broker be used for a large percentage of the Turbot pension plan's trades, with the benefits of commission dollars accruing to the sponsor's employees. In the United States, the Employee Retirement Income Security Act permits a pension plan sponsor—without breaching any fiduciary duty—to use commission dollars to obtain services for the exclusive benefit of the pension plan—but not the sponsor. If Turbot's actions result in benefits for the sponsor's employees rather than the pension plan participants, Turbot's use of these commissions breaches its fiduciary duty to the plan beneficiaries.

In responding to Turbot's request that trades go to a specific broker, Manning must keep in mind that, under Standard IV(B), Interactions with Clients and Prospects, she is required to act in her clients' best interests. As part of acting in her clients' best interests, in trading securities for clients, Manning must ensure that IIA seeks best price and execution. In this context, the plan participants and beneficiaries, not the plan sponsors, are the "clients" of the firm to whom the fiduciary duty is owned.

Responsibilities of Supervisors. As a supervisor, Manning must ensure that IIA employees do not assist violations of the law by acquiescing to the request of Turbot Fisheries Pension Fund or else she will be in violation of Standard III(E), Responsibilities of Supervisors, which requires Manning to exercise reasonable supervision over her employees.

Actions required. Manning should discuss this situation with Barbara Buckley or Buckley's supervisor and explain that this use of plan commission dollars to benefit Turbot is not allowed under U.S. law or fiduciary principles and that neither Manning nor her firm can assist in a violation of the law anywhere in the world. IIA's compliance policies should clearly state the rules for using pension plan commissions within the firm and all its offices.

Manning should enact a policy whereby the use of commission dollars is reviewed periodically—at least annually—to ensure that the use meets the requirements of applicable laws and of IIA's own policies and procedures.

> ***Policy statement for a firm.*** "Employees in a supervisory role are responsible for ensuring that the actions of their employees comply with the firm's policies and procedures and with applicable securities laws and regulations. Any violations or discrepancies should be reported to management or the firm's compliance officer, who should take timely and appropriate action."

Welton and Washington Advisors (A)

Case Facts

Robert Welton's equity management company, Welton Associates, had grown through the years but on a small scale because of the account size of his client base. His clients were a group of 17 portfolios of private individuals and family groups, all of which were managed on a similar basis.

When Welton met Hal Washington at a brokerage conference, they began a friendship that eventually developed into a business relationship. The two men decided to form Welton and Washington Advisors (W&WA) as a registered investment advisory firm, and Welton's clients were transferred to the new firm.

Washington has many institutional contacts from his 25 years of experience as an equity account manager on the sell side (the Wall Street and regional brokerages that sell securities to investment managers, private investors, and others). The two founders divided up the research activities and jointly managed the portfolios.

Welton was comfortable with the firm's past growth, which came primarily from word-of-mouth and formal client referrals, but this pace of growth was not quite enough to support two principals. So, Washington has finally persuaded Welton to expand the firm by emphasizing an institutional clientele, with whom Washington has contacts.

The Growing Organization. When assets under management reach $100 million, including two small ERISA-governed pension fund portfolios, Welton believes they should add additional investment expertise to W&WA. Welton then "puts the word out" to some brokerage contacts that are willing to supply contacts or names of candidates for the additional staff position. Several of the firms offer to help without charge, but California Market Securities states that it will help only if compensated for the service in the form of extra trading commissions.

After several interviews, the person Welton and Washington believe will best fit in with the firm is CFA candidate Jeff Clarkson, who was introduced to Welton by California Market Securities. Clarkson has three years of experience as an equity analyst and has passed Level II of the CFA

This case was written by Glen A. Holden, Jr., CFA, The Capitol Life Insurance Company.

examination. Welton is pleased with the prospect of having a CFA candidate in the firm, and the two founders bring Clarkson on board.

Welton expects to use Clarkson principally as an equity analyst but feels sure he can add other responsibilities as the need arises. Clarkson asks Welton about the AIMR Code of Ethics and Standards of Professional Conduct, and Welton assures him that the firm abides by the Code and Standards.

Welton and Washington now divide the research responsibilities three ways. Each founder takes his favorite sectors or industries, and they give Clarkson the airline, automobile, original equipment manufacturer, and utility industries. Clarkson is somewhat disappointed in his group of companies, partly because of the cyclical nature of their businesses and partly because of the partners' lack of enthusiasm to use issues from these sectors in portfolios. Nonetheless, he is thankful to have a more meaningful position than his previous job and pleased to be working with two well-experienced equity investors.

W&WA does not execute many client trades on a daily basis because of the small sizes of the portfolios. When equity trades do occur, for personal accounts and for client portfolios, W&WA time-stamps all transactions. This practice has been especially useful for the many clients that are family groups, among whom discussions about the securities held in portfolios are frequent and somewhat more candid than among unrelated parties.

Each of the partners sometimes buys small positions for his own portfolio in cases where he has decided the equity of the corporation is too risky for the firm's clients or the company is not large enough to be followed. Their feeling is that just because an investment is found unsuitable for the majority of clients does not mean it is unsuitable for their personal accounts.

Fixed-Income Management. When interest rates were relatively high, Washington and Welton gave little thought to the bonds held in the portfolios. Since interest rates have flattened from a high level and an inverted yield curve, however, the partners have assigned Clarkson the task of reviewing the fixed-income portions of all client portfolios.

Many of the securities are municipal bonds, and Clarkson must make subjective judgments about the taxing authority of the issuing entity and its long-term ability to pay, which gives rise to its credit rating and the yield spread in the marketplace. When Clarkson finished his first review, he commented in writing about the creditworthiness of the issuers and about the call provisions. After Clarkson completed his review, Welton and Washington put him in charge of overseeing the bond portions of the portfolios and, eventually, shifted Clarkson to work entirely on the fixed-income side of the firm.

A drop in both short-term and long-term interest rates, combined with the narrowing of spreads on corporate securities and a change in the slope of the yield curve, presents an unusual opportunity to shorten the portfolios and still achieve the targeted rate of return. During the next several months, Clarkson sells many fixed-income securities from the client accounts, especially the long-dated issues, when they reach acquisition cost and/or call price in order to avoid tax obligations and the risk of early retirement through a call. He places the proceeds in short- and intermediate-term corporate bonds with good call protection. The use of industrial, financial, and utility issues, especially the latter with their higher yields relative to the other two categories, provides additional current income to the portfolios.

Believing that turnover can be expanded to 25 percent a year from the previous 1–2 percent, Clarkson uses large position sizes to facilitate trading. He buys large lots that are then distributed among multiple accounts.

Rates subsequently rise but with a narrowing of spreads. The conservative approach, created in part by client constraints and in part by a lack of experience and general nervousness about long-term interest rates, gives the firm good relative performance each year on the fixed-income side.

> *Several activities at W&WA are or could be in violation of the AIMR Code and Standards. Identify possible violations, state what actions are required by Clarkson and/or the firm to correct the potential violations, and make a short policy statement that a firm could use to prevent the violations.*

Case Discussion

The case discloses possible violations of the Code and Standards involving fair dealing with clients, priority of transactions, portfolio recommendations and actions, reasonable basis and representations, and breach of fiduciary duties.

Priority of Transactions. The partners' personal trading while conducting investment actions for clients is a potential violation of Standard IV(B.4), Priority of Transactions. The fact that the transaction slips are time-stamped does not address the issue of which trades are executed first and whether the partners make available investment opportunities to all clients before making trades for their personal accounts.

Trades for personal accounts in securities that are of no interest to the firm's clients do not violate the Code and Standards. The case implies, however, that sometimes trading is going on in both client accounts and personal accounts ("just because an investment is found unsuitable for the *majority* of clients . . ." [emphasis added]). Whenever one or more client accounts are involved, the partners must refrain from trading for their own account until all client orders have been filled. In no event should they be placing their interests ahead of the clients' or the firm's interests.

Although not specifically required by the Code and Standards, AIMR's Personal Investing Task Force Report (see the topical study titled "Personal Investing" in the *Standards of Practice Handbook*) suggests that, to assure that client trades come first, firms should use such procedures as a "restricted list" (restricting trading until the security is removed from the list) or a moratorium on trading in personal accounts for some period after all client orders have been filled.

In addition, under Standard IV(B.7), Disclosure of Conflicts to Clients and Prospects, Robert Welton and Hal Washington have an obligation to disclose beneficial ownership of securities and other matters that might affect or impair the partners' judgments regarding investment recommendations.

Actions required. The principals and employees at Welton and Washington Advisors must cease transacting in securities for their own accounts while any client orders for those securities remain unfilled. W&WA should implement policies to ensure that client orders are given priority.

Policy statement for a firm. "In all events, the interests of the firm's clients will come before those of the firm itself or those of its employees.

"Employees are prohibited from trading in securities (or derivatives thereof) that are being purchased or sold from client portfolios until 72 hours have passed from the completion of all orders. Employees wishing to trade in securities that are also being traded in client accounts must request approval from the firm in advance and in writing. They will be cleared to trade only after all client orders have been satisfied and the applicable time restriction has passed."

Portfolio Management. The case description of Jeff Clarkson's activities raises questions about violations of Standard IV(B.2), Portfolio Investment Recommendations and Actions, and Standard IV(A.1), Reasonable Basis and Representations.

▪ *Portfolio recommendations and actions.* Standard IV(B.2) begins by stating that an AIMR member shall "make a reasonable inquiry into a client's . . . investment objectives prior to making any investment recommendations and shall update this information as necessary, but no less frequently than annually. . . ." Clarkson, as a CFA candidate, should be aware of his responsibility to the clients prior to taking any action with regards to a portfolio.

W&WA has apparently not laid out client guidelines, nor has the firm updated guidelines. The clients' investment objectives and any periodic review have both been neglected. Clarkson should have updated the files on all clients before replacing securities in client portfolios. The consideration of, in the words of Standard IV(B.2), "applicable relevant factors" will determine the appropriateness and suitability of his fixed-income actions for each client portfolio.

The adaptation of a portfolio to changing environments is prudent management. The case describes a disregard for clients, however, in these activities. Changes in investment strategy should be communicated *in advance* to the clients so that the manager can reach a decision as to the appropriateness and suitability of the investment with the client's full knowledge and consent. Agreement "after the fact" does not allow for a dialogue between the investment manager and the client.

Changing strategy to increase after-tax income may be in keeping with the client's investment objectives, but the sale of securities to accomplish this end may not be in keeping with client guidelines. Also, changing market conditions generally prevent a generalization in terms of after-tax yield, so corporate securities may meet this objective at certain times but not at all times. Finally, the discussion does not suggest that clients have been contacted in regard to the increased turnover in their portfolios.

▨ *Reasonable basis and representations.* The requirement that members have a reasonable and adequate basis for investment recommendations can be met only if Clarkson has updated the client files and reviewed the investment guidelines for each portfolio, discussing changes from prior practice with the clients and receiving their consent in advance. Clarkson should direct his attention to the issue of proper selection of securities for inclusion in the portfolios. Each of the corporate issuers should be reviewed in the context of security selection and effect on portfolio diversification.

Actions required. Clarkson must first review the client files and make direct contact with the clients to ensure that all information in the files is current. The investment objectives of the clients, the after-tax return on fixed-income securities, turnover, and other considerations are appropriate topics of discussion. He should then review the securities held in client portfolios.

Once portfolio objectives and constraints have been finalized and the risks of securities described in detail to the client beforehand, Clarkson can then make recommendations for investment or replacement securities in client portfolios. Clarkson should keep written records documenting the rationale for the investment recommendations and the research he carried out to justify the recommendations.

Policy statement for a firm. "Investment objectives for each account will be written and communicated to all investment personnel. The firm will review all client portfolios and investment policy statements internally every six months and with the client every year.

"Changes in investment strategy will be communicated to the client in advance of any action in order to fully review the firm's thinking in this regard with the client and to gain the client's concurrence. Differences of opinion will be resolved to the client's satisfaction before implementation of any investment action.

"Portfolio investment recommendations will be made only after a thorough review of the investment and its suitability for client portfolios. Files will be kept updated while individual securities are held in a portfolio and for a period of one year after the last of an issue is sold."

Fiduciary Duties. If Welton and Washington agreed to the demand of California Market Securities to provide "extra trading commissions" as compensation for an employee referral, they violated Standard IV(B.1), Fiduciary Duties, when they hired Clarkson. They used (or misappropriated) client funds for the firm's benefit; rather than pay directly for a service, Welton was obtaining a benefit for the firm at the expense of the firm's clients. Welton and Washington must demonstrate that they do not favor W&WA or the brokerage firm over their clients.

Actions required. If W&WA obligated itself to pay California Market Securities for services rendered on behalf of W&WA in finding Clarkson, the firm must negotiate the dollar amount and terms and pay California Market Securities directly rather than in the form of commissions.

Policy statement for a firm. "The firm will manage client portfolios for the sole benefit of its clients. Execution of client trades will be performed within this guideline. Client assets will be used only to provide benefit to the clients and their portfolios."

Welton and Washington Advisors (B)

Case Facts

Robert Welton and Hal Washington are pleased by Jeff Clarkson's willingness to take charge of the fixed-income portion of the portfolios because they want to concentrate on managing the equity portions. With the favorable performance in the fixed-income portions, they begin to rely on and tout Clarkson's analytical and management capabilities in new business presentations and Requests for Proposals.

When Clarkson successfully completes the CFA series of examinations and is awarded his CFA charter, he advances to a more senior role in the firm. Flush with success over both the good performance of the fixed-income portfolios and the prestige of his new position, Clarkson decides that his next steps should be to move into portfolio strategy.

Clarkson has considered various ideas in professional journals that might add value to the portfolios, including a strategy of enhancing portfolio coupon income to obtain better relative returns for the same average maturity. The articles described the benefits and default risk associated with high-yield securities (fixed-income securities whose issuers are rated below investment grade by one or more of the major rating agencies, such as Moody's Investor Service or Standard and Poor's Ratings Group). Some of these issues come from formerly high-quality industrial and utility companies that have fallen from investment-grade status because of business difficulties. He begins to invest in these "fallen angels" for Welton and Washington Advisors portfolios.

At about the same time, Clarkson is approached by Craig Stout, one of the investment bankers at Logan Larimer, an old-line Wall Street firm. Logan Larimer underwrites securities of spin-offs from corporate reorganizations and companies getting beyond venture capital financing. These companies typically have a need for additional equity in this transition. Many of them thus offer rights, warrants, or stocks bundled into a unit with their debt securities. With their thin capitalization and/or heavy debt burden in relation to their capital base, these companies' securities are classified by the ratings agencies as below investment grade.

Clarkson realizes that these securities could fit with the use of other high-

This case was written by Glen A. Holden, Jr., CFA, The Capitol Life Insurance Company.

yield issues in the corporate sector of the W&WA client portfolios. He remains skeptical, however, because either the ratings of the former parents no longer apply or the emerging companies do not have rating histories.

Talking to Clarkson, Stout disparages the rating agencies and the term "junk bonds" often used to describe the securities. He points out that Logan Larimer has its own analytical staff and traders to trade in the secondary markets and can thus alleviate any concerns about the continued creditworthiness of an issuer. In addition, Logan Larimer's due diligence team makes an initial, in-depth review of each company. "Furthermore," he says, "the firm only accepts clients that are known to us—those where we have some relationship with the principals in the transaction. With this personal contact, our customers feel more comfortable with the business aspects of the deal."

Stout would like to bring W&WA on as a customer. He suggests that Clarkson look over a couple of the newest offerings and talk to Logan Larimer's research staff, and perhaps the Logan Larimer traders, to get a sense of how recently issued securities have traded in the aftermarket. Clarkson takes this opportunity to review with the Logan and Larimer staff the securities of several Logan Larimer offering companies: Wazee Specialty Steel, Lincoln Enter-Cable, and Wynkoop Software. Although he has a favorable impression of the spin-offs, he still prefers using the lower-rated securities of established companies.

In another attempt to gain access to W&WA, Stout offers to give Clarkson "first look" at a new underwriting of a debt issue with warrants attached involving the Argyle & Checker Company. Clarkson reviews the most recent research report prepared by Logan Larimer on the company, the 10-K, and the prospectus. Two days later, Stout calls Clarkson and suggests he open accounts at Logan Larimer for W&WA's clients and senior employees. Clarkson analyzes the Logan Larimer information and concludes that the company's bonds might be a worthwhile investment.

Prior to the offering of the Argyle & Checker Company debt units, Stout invites Clarkson to a special private meeting with Argyle & Checker's senior management at its plant. After a lengthy tour of the modernized facility, the company's chief financial officer becomes quite chatty with the group and discusses a variety of information about the future of the company, including expansion plans and future earnings projections. Clarkson decides this venture is very desirable and places orders for his client portfolios and his own newly established account.

In their next conversation, Stout talks about cooperation being two-sided and about Logan Larimer's close relationships with institutional clients, many of which use outside investment advisors for the management of their pension and profit-sharing funds and look to Logan Larimer for advice when replacing existing managers. Stout also invites Clarkson to an exclusive retreat for senior executives at Logan Larimer's expense and offers him a private bungalow at the next Logan Larimer research conference.

> *Several activities at W&WA are or could be in violation of the AIMR Code of Ethics and Standards of Professional Conduct. Identify possible violations, state what actions are required of Clarkson and his firm to correct the potential violations, and make a short policy statement a firm could use to prevent the violations.*

Case Discussion

Unscrupulous business approaches can make questionable activities seem reasonable and appealing. This case discloses violations or possible violations of the AIMR Code and Standards involving use of material nonpublic information, independence and objectivity, and reasonable basis and representations.

Material Nonpublic Information. Logan Larimer has access to material nonpublic information through its special relationships with individuals at the helms of the companies dealing with its investment banking division. Therefore, through the contact with the investment bankers at Logan Larimer, their due diligence and research staff, and the Logan Larimer traders responsible for making markets in the securities, Jeff Clarkson runs a significant risk of coming into contact with material nonpublic information.

The tour of the Argyle & Checker Company plant is an excellent example of Clarkson's exposure to inside information that is selectively disclosed by a company. Clarkson's use of this information, in whatever form, would be a violation of Standard V(A), Prohibition against Use of Material Nonpublic Information. If Clarkson placed orders with Logan Larimer to his and his clients' benefit on the basis of material nonpublic information, he was violating Standard V(A).

Furthermore, Standard V(A) requires that if Clarkson believes he is in possession of material nonpublic information, he must take steps to achieve public dissemination of the information, which as a practical matter, and in the midst of an underwriting of securities, may be extremely difficult. Because of this difficulty, the most appropriate procedure is for senior members of the firm to take steps to bring about disclosure of the material nonpublic information.

Actions required. Clarkson must refrain from transacting in securities on the basis of material nonpublic information.

Policy statement for a firm. "Firm employees who believe they have come in contact with material nonpublic information should refrain from trading securities on the basis of that information and should present the circumstances of the contact to the senior members of the firm for review. Attempts to force dissemination shall be conducted by the firm, not by any one individual."

Independence and Objectivity. The case describes a number of violations of Standard IV(A.3), Independence and Objectivity. The first involves a bold attempt by Craig Stout to garner favor with Clarkson and influence Clarkson's decision making. Clarkson should be extremely careful in any acceptance of a "first look" at securities being underwritten by Logan Larimer. If the issues are being made available only to selected Logan Larimer clients, he is exposing himself to selective disclosure violations, as noted in the previous section.

Stout's introduction of Clarkson to some of Logan Larimer's institutional relationships (with thinly veiled hints that something might be done to influence decisions to favor W&WA), offer of exclusive management retreats and preferred accommodations at meetings, and establishment of personal accounts for hot issues are actions by Logan Larimer in an aggressive program to gain the business of W&WA. Accepting these perquisites would cast serious doubt on Clarkson's ability to maintain his independence and objectivity.

Actions required. Clarkson must reject the flagrant attempts on the part of Stout and Logan Larimer to gain favor and influence his decision making. He should turn down special opportunities and other advantages that would not be offered to others.

Policy statement for a firm. "Employees are prohibited from accepting special favors intended to influence business decisions and other gifts that exceed US$100. When traveling on business matters to an event sponsored by a corporate issuer of securities or its investment banking firm, employees may not accept transportation, meals, accommodations, or other benefits that could interfere with the employee's independence."

Reasonable Basis and Representations. In making potentially faulty or self-interested investment decisions to use securities underwritten by Logan Larimer on the basis of Logan Larimer's recommendation alone, Clarkson has violated Standard IV(A.1), Reasonable Basis and Representations. Clarkson has a duty to conduct his own research or rely on independent and objective sources. Clarkson must not be swayed by a slick presentation or predigested financial information presented by Logan

Larimer. Because the brokerage firm has a vested interest in the purchase of the securities, basing a decision solely on the Logan Larimer research violates the trust placed by clients in W&WA.

Actions required. In order to fulfill his duty to the W&WA clients, Clarkson must not make any decisions about securities offered by Logan and Larimer until he has made reasonable efforts to use adequate, unbiased information independent of Logan Larimer's self-interested analysis.

> ***Policy statement for a firm.*** "Employees shall exercise diligence and thoroughness in making investment recommendations or taking investment actions and shall have a reasonable and adequate basis, supported by appropriate research and investigation, for making any investment recommendations or taking investment actions."

Welton and Washington Advisors (C)

Case Facts

As interest rates move down to historically low levels, Jeff Clarkson, CFA, feeling quite nervous, talks to Robert Welton about the potential for an adverse interest rate environment. Welton's response is to reiterate his confidence in Clarkson's abilities and remind him that "the clients are counting on you."

Clarkson reviews all of the accounts again for, among other things, their investment objectives, trading constraints, and fees paid to the firm. He is concerned that the institutional clients added in the recent years through Hal Washington's efforts, which have not had close contact with Welton and Washington Advisors or a long relationship with Welton or Washington through a variety of market cycles, will become impatient with poor returns. The clients often call to see how their portfolios are doing relative to the market and their own benchmarks, particularly when there are major down drafts in the market. In addition, for the consultants that oversee the newer institutional accounts, the time periods in which they assess performance have grown shorter and shorter. Clarkson realizes that the transition from investing for the long term for individual investors to investing for quarterly performance is not as easy as the staff at W&WA once expected.

In anticipation of rising rates, Clarkson identifies fixed-income securities that should be sold from newer clients' accounts, with the proceeds to be reinvested in two-year U.S. Treasury securities in order to shorten the duration of the portfolios. He prepares the bid lists and initiates the sell program. When rates rise 30 basis points two weeks later, he identifies another round of bonds to be sold from various portfolios and again executes the trades himself.

W&WA has by this time added a staff person in the administrative area, Margaret Blake-Court. As she is finalizing the reporting of the security sales and the subsequent reinvestment of proceeds, she notices that all the sales in the first round of Clarkson's trades were from client portfolios monitored by third-party consultants for the portfolios' relative performance. Blake-Court suspects that Clarkson is trying to keep in the good graces of the consultants

This case was written by Glen A. Holden, Jr., CFA, The Capitol Life Insurance Company.

by focusing his attention on the quarterly performance for the newer, total rate of return portfolios. She recognizes that the second round involved those accounts that pay the highest gross fees to the firm. Margaret decides she must bring these facts to the attention of Welton.

When Welton raises the issue of the preferential trading with Clarkson, Clarkson argues that "each account has different investment objectives, so naturally, each will be managed differently." Welton remains suspicious, however, and begins to check on the management of the fixed-income portfolios.

After investigating the actions taken on behalf of clients, Welton asks for copies of Clarkson's brokerage statements and the trade confirmations. In reviewing the confirmations, Welton notices that when the Argyle & Checker bond units were purchased for client portfolios, they were delivered to W&WA client portfolios as brokered transactions without the warrants that were originally offered with the bond units. Curious about the lack of the warrants in the client portfolios, Welton calls Logan Larimer. Craig Stout offers the explanation that W&WA elected to keep the warrants. "This did not affect the prospectus or the financial information contained in it," he continues, "because the warrants were not assigned any value. So, purchases made for W&WA client portfolios were brokered transactions."

Welton discovers that all the units purchased from Logan Larimer, both for client portfolios and Clarkson's own account, flowed through Clarkson's account. Clarkson's activity log shows the purchase of the debt units as a principal transaction and the simultaneous sale of the bonds as a brokered transaction, with both the "buys" and "sells" crossing at the same price. The warrants remained in Clarkson's account, while the high-yield securities, stripped of the warrants, were delivered to the client portfolios.

When confronted by Welton, Clarkson states that his understanding is that the securities laws address only equity securities and related instruments. Because the issues were bonds, Clarkson does not believe he violated any rules.

Later, Welton learns that Clarkson has another Logan Larimer debt-and-warrants deal in the works. Welton fears that this deal will be handled like the others and if he does not challenge Clarkson, he stands a good chance of being an unwilling participant in multiple ethical violations. But Welton's decision about what to do and how to proceed in his dealings with Clarkson is complicated by the fact that many recent client additions came to the firm because of the founders touting Clarkson's skills and these customers have come to rely on Clarkson. With these clients, Clarkson has supplanted Washington as the primary client contact. If Clarkson is dismissed or reprimanded harshly enough that he leaves, the firm could lose some of these clients.

Several activities at W&WA are or could be in violation of the AIMR Code of Ethics and Standards of Professional Conduct. Identify violations, state what actions are required by Clarkson or Welton to correct the potential violations, and make a short policy statement that a firm could use to prevent such violations.

Case Discussion

When standards appear loose or monitoring is lax, supervisors run the risk of becoming unwilling partners in ethical (and legal) violations. This case discloses possible violations of the AIMR Code and Standards relating to fundamental responsibilities, professional conduct, fiduciary duties, portfolio investment actions, fair dealing, priority of transactions, independence and objectivity, and responsibilities of supervisors.

Fundamental Responsibilities, Professional Misconduct, and Fiduciary Duties. Jeff Clarkson has engaged in a series of actions that violate the Code of Ethics and a number of the Standards. The pattern of dishonesty and deceit represented by the transactions with Logan Larimer are clear violations of Standard II(B), Professional Misconduct. By attempting to justify his actions on the basis that bond trades are not regulated as are transactions in equity securities, Clarkson demonstrates his failure to maintain knowledge of and comply with all applicable laws and regulations, in violation of his responsibilities as an investment professional under Standard I, Fundamental Responsibilities.

By keeping the warrants in his Logan Larimer account, Clarkson accepted nonmonetary compensation that could be exchanged for cash upon the sale of the warrants. He was thus taking part of the economic value that should rightfully belong to his clients. Therefore, keeping the warrants is a breach of the duty he owes those clients, which violates Standard IV(B.1), Fiduciary Duties. Even assuming that his first receipt of the warrants stripped from the debt units through a trade with Logan Larimer was an administrative error by Logan Larimer's back office or took place as a result of a mistake in judgment, Clarkson's willful and continued acceptance of the warrants was unethical and illegal and reflected adversely on the investment profession. Clarkson could be disciplined by Welton and Washington Advisors and AIMR and could face a criminal prosecution. Clarkson cannot continue to engage in transactions that benefit him personally at the expense of W&WA clients.

Actions required. Clarkson should direct Logan Larimer to reverse the transactions going through his account, and he should distribute the warrants or their value on a pro rata basis to the W&WA client portfolios affected.

Policy statement for a firm. "Employees will follow the AIMR Code of Ethics and Standards of Professional Conduct. Illegal or unethical behavior is a negative reflection upon the firm and the profession and will not be tolerated. Such behavior will be immediate grounds for termination of employment. All employees are charged with the responsibility to maintain the integrity of the firm in dealings with clients and the general public."

Fair Dealing. Clarkson violated Standard IV(B.3), Fair Dealing, by engaging in preferential trading on behalf of performance-oriented and high-fee accounts. All clients are entitled to fair treatment by the firm. When Clarkson acted to shorten the duration of the performance-oriented portfolios, he was potentially giving those accounts an unfair advantage at the expense of other W&WA discretionary accounts with similar objectives. The same is true when he singled out the highest-paying accounts for preferential treatment. W&WA must not allow its employees to breach their duties to the firm's clients and to the firm itself.

Actions required. Clarkson must begin giving similar treatment to all accounts with similar investment objectives.

Policy statement for a firm. "The highest responsibility of employees of the firm is to meet the fiduciary duties owed to clients in the management of their assets. All employees will keep this important part of the firm's mission statement in mind when making investment recommendations or taking portfolio action."

Independence, Objectivity, and Disclosure of Conflicts. Clarkson's trading activity through Logan Larimer violated Standard IV(A.3), Independence and Objectivity. Clarkson's independence and objectivity with respect to securities offered by Logan Larimer are called into question by his receipt of indirect compensation in the form of warrants from Logan Larimer.

Furthermore, Clarkson is obliged to disclose to his employer and to clients all matters that might reasonably be expected to impair his ability to render objective and unbiased opinions. By failing to disclose the compensation received from Logan Larimer, Clarkson violated Standard III(C), Disclosure of Conflicts to Employer, and Standard IV(B.7), Disclosure of Conflicts to Clients and Prospects.

Actions required. W&WA should prohibit all employees from accepting direct or indirect compensation from any party when the acceptance of the compensation creates an actual or perceived conflict of interest with W&WA clients.

Policy statement for a firm. "Conflicts of interest that may lead to an inability to render objective advice are prohibited. All employees are expected to maintain their independence and objectivity in their relationships with parties outside the firm."

Responsibilities of Supervisors. As principals of the firm and Clarkson's supervisors, Welton and Washington are obliged to exercise reasonable supervision of Clarkson's actions. They may have violated Standard III(E), Responsibilities of Supervisors, by failing to have procedures in place to detect activities such as Clarkson's trading. On being informed of Clarkson's previous course of action and the fact that Clarkson may be planning similar activities in connection with an upcoming Logan Larimer deal, Welton and Washington's continued inaction clearly violates their obligation to exercise reasonable supervision to prevent violations of applicable laws and the Code and Standards. Welton and Washington have the ultimate responsibility to manage and control the actions of employees of the firm or, in the language of Standard III(E), "to influence the conduct of others." Whatever benefits Clarkson provides the firm are immaterial in terms of Welton's duty to the firm's clientele and to his associates and subordinates at the firm. The decision to confront Clarkson may be difficult, but it is necessary for Welton to challenge Clarkson and eliminate a weighty problem, either by removing Clarkson's responsibilities or terminating his employment at W&WA.

Actions required. Welton must confront Clarkson about Clarkson's activities and should monitor his trading (or implement a procedure by which a compliance officer or some other designated party is responsible for monitoring trading). Welton should take appropriate disciplinary action, including the termination of Clarkson in the event of further violations.

Welton should adopt policies and procedures designed to ensure compliance with applicable laws and detect violations such as those committed by Clarkson. Failure to comply with the firm's policies and procedures should result in appropriate disciplinary action by the firm, including suspension and termination of employment when warranted. Welton needs to implement a program of employee training in the firm's compliance obligations. W&WA should provide employees a compliance manual when they are hired and should require that it be read during the first day and that employees sign an affirmation that they understand the manual.

Policy statement for a firm. "Employees with supervisory responsibility, including the ability or authority to influence the conduct of any other employee, shall exercise reasonable supervision of those within their authority to prevent violations of applicable statutes, regulations, and provisions of the Code and Standards."

Velstar Capital Management

Case Facts

Mike Mason, an analyst with Velstar Capital Management, is unsure about which course of action he should take. He suspects that Sam Richardson, one of the firm's portfolio managers, is making transactions of questionable merit on behalf of his clients in order to profit personally. Mason does not have specific proof, however, and has been in hot water with this manager in the past. He is not sure how the firm president would react if told, but he believes that if he makes an accusation that is later deemed to be without merit, he could lose his job.

Background. Velstar Capital Management is a money management firm that specializes in small-capitalization stocks. The firm's main clientele are small- and medium-sized pension funds. Velstar was started in 1981 by John Veldine, CFA, who remains the company president. In 1988, Gerald Page was named vice president of the company. Veldine and Page currently own all of Velstar's equity and share management responsibilities. In addition to the two principals, three portfolio managers are involved with making investment decisions: Richardson, Janette Rigby, CFA, and Thomas McClellan.

Richardson, having joined the firm in 1989, is the most senior of the three and is regarded as a competent manager with an outstanding flair for developing and maintaining clientele. Veldine has often lauded Richardson's success with clients, and the two men have also become close friends. Indeed, rumors have been circulating around Velstar that Richardson is likely to be named a third principal.

Mike Mason. Mason, 27 years old, is one of eight analysts employed at Velstar. He received an M.B.A. in May of the previous year and left graduate school with a strong desire to work in the investment industry. He performed well in the M.B.A. program and received one offer for an assistant treasurer's position and two offers to work as a commercial lender, but he had difficulty obtaining an interview with a money management firm, trust division, or insurance company. He was almost ready to accept a commercial lending position when he met Rigby, who was a guest speaker for the student finance club.

Rigby was impressed by Mason's knowledge and desire to work in

---

This case was written by Scott L. Lummer, CFA, Ibbotson Associates; case discussion by Douglas R. Hughes, CFA.

investments, so she convinced her colleagues to grant Mason an interview. After Mason's visit to Velstar, the firm offered him an analyst position.

Mason has worked for Velstar for 18 months. During the first 10 months, he worked primarily on assignments for Rigby. He developed a sincere respect for her thoroughness in conducting research, her diligent work ethic, and her steady management style. Rigby spoke to Mason often about the benefits of obtaining the CFA designation. With her encouragement, he decided to join the local AIMR society of financial analysts, as well as AIMR, and to enroll in the CFA candidate program.

The Initial Conflict. Ten months ago, in March, Richardson began frequently requesting that Mason be assigned to him for analytical assistance. Richardson often asked Mason to perform due diligence work on initial public offerings (IPOs) that Richardson was considering for his clients' portfolios. Many times, explaining that he had already checked most of the relevant information, Richardson asked Mason to investigate only specific facets of an IPO. In those cases, Richardson wanted a simple summary from Mason stating whether any concerns based on those facets existed, and he briefly reviewed the aspects Mason had checked.

Richardson was much more demanding than Rigby was, and he often became agitated if he considered Mason to be too deliberate or did not agree with Mason's conclusions. Richardson never criticized Mason in public, however, and often heaped strong praise on Mason in front of colleagues. In fact, in Mason's 12-month employment review, Richardson described Mason as the single most impressive analyst he had observed at Velstar. Mason became more and more impressed with Richardson's enthusiasm for the job.

As a result of his performance review in July, Mason received a raise of $25,000. He and Nadine, his wife of five years, celebrated his good fortune by purchasing a $150,000 house. In addition, deciding they could now live off his salary alone for a few years, they resolved to start a family. Nadine became pregnant in September and planned to resign from her position as a manager of a franchised restaurant in the coming April.

Last month, Richardson asked Mason to investigate some aspects of an IPO of Bowman Software. In conversation, Richardson mentioned that one of the portfolios for which this stock was being considered was the pension plan of a computer manufacturer. Later, considering that one objective of pension fund management is to diversify employees' risk, Mason wondered about the advisability of including the stock of a software developer in the pension plan of a company in essentially the same industry. Mason had learned in the Level I readings for the CFA exam about the benefits of diversification. After pondering this issue, he mentioned it to Richardson, who snapped, "Since when is it the role of a junior analyst to debate portfolio suitability?"

The next day, Mason went to Rigby's office and asked her a generic question about purchasing the stock of a company in a related industry for a pension fund. She answered that, in her opinion, it would not be appropriate, and she gave Mason a copy of a recent *Financial Analysts Journal*® containing an article supporting her stand. Bolstered by Rigby's agreement with his position, Mason went to Richardson's office and reiterated his position. When he handed Richardson a copy of the supporting article, Richardson went berserk—tearing the article to pieces and screaming at Mason, "Your career will be in the same condition as this article if you continue to stick your nose where it doesn't belong!"

Later that week, Mason was returning from lunch when Veldine walked into the same elevator. Veldine asked how things were going, and Mason responded that he hoped he could "get out of Richardson's doghouse." Veldine asked what the problem was, but Mason said it was not a major issue. Veldine asked him again, however, saying that he would not discuss the issue with Richardson. Mason then described the debate and his view that the investment was inappropriate for the computer company's fund. Veldine told Mason not to worry, that Richardson was very excitable and it would soon blow over.

Two hours later, Richardson called Mason into his office, slammed a document down on his desk, and told Mason to read the highlighted text. The document was a report, dated two days previously, on the purchase of Bowman for the pension fund. The highlighted text said, "Although we usually do not recommend a stock in an industry similar to that of the plan sponsor for inclusion in the fund, our belief is that this stock is severely undervalued. Hence, in our opinion, weighing the risk and return objectives for the plan, the welfare of the plan's participants is best served by the purchase of Bowman's stock."

Richardson said, "I hope you're now satisfied. You're not the only person who knows about diversification of pension fund portfolios. I agree that, in general, this stock would not be an appropriate purchase, but in this case, because I believed the stock was so deeply undervalued, I decided to add it to the portfolio. Moreover, this should have been a matter that was kept between the two of us. I don't appreciate being told by Mr. Veldine that I need to get control over my analysts. If you ever go over my head again, you're finished!"

Later that afternoon, Rigby called Mason into her office and told him that during an Investment Committee Meeting, Richardson had been ranting to her and McClellan about Mason "running around me to Veldine." She urged Mason to be careful around Richardson. Three years ago, an analyst who had been fired ostensibly for sloppy work was, in all likelihood, fired because he had occasionally challenged Richardson's opinions. She said Richardson had also set out on a vendetta, vowing that the fired analyst would never work in the industry again. To Rigby's knowledge, Richardson had kept that vow.

The Current Situation. In the next few weeks, tensions between Mason and Richardson eased. One day in mid-November, Richardson summoned Mason to his office and said, "Mike, I think one of the reasons we had a conflict over the Bowman stock was that you are seeing a very limited piece of the overall analytical process. For any IPO that we consider, we perform a detailed discounted cash flow valuation. I've been doing all of the valuation work myself, but it may be helpful to both of us for you to do some of this work. What do you know about DCF valuation?"

Mason told Richardson about covering the topic in the CFA curriculum and performing DCF analyses on some valuation software that Velstar had purchased for an assignment he was working on for Rigby. Richardson then gave Mason a file on the IPO of Corwin Pies, a dessert foods company that would be offered next week to the market at a price of $17 a share. Richardson asked him to perform some general due diligence work and to determine whether $17 was an appropriate price based on a list of assumptions Richardson had prepared.

After conducting his due diligence, Mason began entering the valuation assumptions in the computer. He agreed with the assumptions Richardson had prepared except for those for cost of goods sold (COGS) and sales growth. Richardson had projected COGS to decline by 0.5 percent each year in the first 10 years. He had forecasted sales growth to average 23 percent a year for the first 10 years, which Mason believed was too high.

Mason then investigated the performance of other snack and dessert foods companies in their first 10 years after being publicly traded. He found that, on average, COGS *increased* slightly during the first few years and then leveled off. Sales typically grew at a rate of 20–30 percent during the first five years and then fell to the industry's average growth, which is currently forecasted to be approximately 8 percent.

With this information, Mason entered new assumptions for sales growth and COGS that he believed were more reasonable than Richardson's. The resulting valuation estimate was $14.89 a share. After performing some sensitivity analysis, Mason decided that an appropriate range was between $12.50 and $17.75 a share.

To satisfy his curiosity, he then entered Richardson's original assumptions. The resulting estimate was $22.71, with a range between $20.00 and $25.50. Mason was delighted; he believed his extra effort was justified because it led to a different decision regarding the stock. Mason prepared a report that briefly described his conclusions and the basis for the change in assumptions and left the report on Richardson's desk.

The next morning, Richardson called Mason into his office and asked him to repeat Richardson's original instructions. He then asked if he had specifically asked Mason to verify any of the assumptions. When Mason replied that Richardson had not, Richardson said, "Someday, you will be a portfolio manager and you will be able to make these assumptions on your own. However, if you ever want to reach that point at this firm, you better start listening to directions. Now, turn in a report using the assumptions I gave you." Mason responded that doing so would lead to a different conclusion regarding the stock. Richardson said that, in that case, it was even more important that Mason use the assumptions Richardson gave him.

Mason went back to the computer and reentered the original assumptions. As he did so, however, he began to wonder if this company had some specific characteristic that he was ignoring that would lead to the more optimistic scenario projected by Richardson. He obtained the complete file on Corwin Pies and began to read through the prospectus. He noticed that the lead underwriter of the IPO was Weston, Elliott and Company; the name jogged his memory because he thought that was the same investment bank that had underwritten the Bowman IPO. In fact, he seemed to recall that many of the IPOs he had analyzed had Weston, Elliott as an underwriter.

That evening, he pulled the files on all of the IPOs he had analyzed in the past year. Indeed, 7 of these 15 IPOs, including the Corwin and Bowman stocks, had been underwritten by Weston, Elliott. He was interested to note that, with the exception of Corwin, all were purchased for at least one of Richardson's clients. Of the other 8 IPOs, only 2 were deemed acceptable for investment for any of Velstar's clients.

He realized something else unusual. The seven Weston, Elliott IPOs were the ones for which Richardson claimed he had already performed most of the due diligence and asked Mason to investigate only a few specific features. The files showed no investigation other than Mason's, however; the only support for the transactions listed in the files was Richardson's valuation analyses and Mason's limited due diligence analyses. The files also contained no mention that Richardson had asked Mason to carry out limited investigations. Mason believed the analyses were too narrow to justify any purchase recommendations, and he was worried that the files made him appear lax in carrying out the due diligence work.

Further research of the seven Weston, Elliott IPOs showed that the cover letter for each prospectus was signed by the same investment banker, Keith Marshall. Mason found the letters from Marshall to be more friendly and less descriptive of the IPO than the cover letters he read from the other underwriters.

The Dilemma. Now Mason is lying awake wondering what to do. Richardson is expecting a valuation analysis in the morning supporting the purchase of Corwin. Mason knows from a conversation with Rigby that only about 25 percent of IPOs considered by Velstar are purchased for client portfolios. He can conceive of no business reason why the Weston, Elliott deals were better than the other IPOs or why they should have been less thoroughly researched. He suspects that Richardson has somehow been profiting from these deals, but he has no specific evidence. He believes he should take some action—but what action and how should he proceed?

> *Identify the possible violations of the Code of Ethics and Standards of Professional Conduct in the case and describe the issues confronting Mason. What are Mason's alternatives with respect to the situation? Discuss policies a firm could use to prevent the kinds of problems revealed in the case.*

Case Discussion

The Velstar case describes risks and ethical dilemmas not only to Mike Mason, the central figure, but to the firm itself. Conflicting emotions and value judgments concerning appropriate actions are prevalent throughout this case. The problems range in seriousness from what could be characterized as an isolated dispute between an analyst and a portfolio manager to potential wrongdoing by a senior employee of the firm to systematic collusion in that wrongdoing by the firm principals.

The fact that the situation has progressed this far is an indication of organizational trouble and management failure. The careers of two professionals may be in jeopardy, and disregard for the firm's clients is in evidence. Failure to have in place prescribed procedures to allow for prompt and appropriate resolution of such issues threatens the position of well-intentioned employees, strains working relationships, facilitates wrongdoing, and undermines the overall ethical climate of the firm.

Mason's views of wrongdoing are largely presumptive at this juncture. He has enough "evidence," however, to warrant suspicion and is correct to raise questions. The Code and Standards provide all members with an ethical framework from which to perform their duties and, perhaps as important, provide a measure of assurance to individuals and firms served by the investment profession.

AIMR's Standards of Conduct. Because incontrovertible evidence of wrongdoing is not presented, specific violations cannot be determined with any certainty. The Standards of Professional Conduct that are involved in this situation, however, can be identified.

▓ *Standard I, Fundamental Responsibilities.* Are the lead characters in this case knowledgeable and in compliance with all applicable laws, rules, and regulations and AIMR's Code and Standards? By following Sam Richardson's directives, is Mason participating in or assisting in acts that violate applicable laws, rules, or regulations, including AIMR's Standards?

▓ *Standard III(A), Obligation to Inform Employer of Code and Standards.* Has Mason informed Richardson and Velstar's principals that he is obligated to comply with AIMR Standards and is subject to disciplinary sanctions for violations?

▓ *Standard III(C), Disclosure of Conflicts to Employer.* Does a conflict of interest exist by virtue of a special relationship between Richardson and Weston, Elliott and Company, the investment banking firm (or perhaps between Velstar and Weston, Elliott), and if so, has it been disclosed?

▓ *Standard III(E), Responsibilities of Supervisors.* Is reasonable supervision being exercised at Velstar by Richardson? By John Veldine and Gerald Page?

▓ *Standard IV(A.1), Reasonable Basis and Representations.* Are the investment actions for clients based on diligent and thorough research? Do investment recommendations and actions have a reasonable and adequate basis?

Is Richardson maintaining appropriate records to support the reasonableness of his investment actions? Do supporting records even exist?

▓ *Standard IV(A.2), Research Reports.* Is Mason using reasonable judgment and including relevant factors in preparing research reports? Is Richardson?

▓ *Standard IV(A.3), Independence and Objectivity.* Is Mason exercising independence and objectivity by complying with Richardson's request to prepare his report so that it conforms to predetermined conclusions?

▓ *Standard IV(B.1), Fiduciary Duties.* Has Richardson used care in following applicable fiduciary duties (by acting for the exclusive benefit of plan participants and beneficiaries, for example)?

▓ *Standard IV(B.2), Portfolio Investment Recommendations and Actions.* Is Richardson properly taking into account the needs and circumstances of his clients when he purchases the stock of various IPOs for his accounts?

▓ *Standard IV(B.4), Priority of Transactions.* In taking investment actions, is Richardson (or any other member of the firm) placing his own interests above those of his clients?

▓ *Standard IV(B.8), Disclosure of Referral Fees.* Is Richardson receiving any compensation or other benefits as a result of his relationship with Weston, Elliott? If so, have such arrangements been disclosed?

What Mason Needs to Consider. Once Mason has knowledge of activities he believes violate ethical principles (including the Code and Standards) or securities laws, he needs to consider the following factors in deciding on an appropriate course of action.

▧ *Obligation as an employee.* Mason's role as an employee of Velstar carries with it certain obligations and expectations. He has a duty to act in good faith and perform in ways that further the firm's business interests. As with any obligation, however, certain conditions may exist that would release him from an obligation of unyielding loyalty. For example, if he is asked to participate in illegal or unethical activities, Mason must refuse.

▧ *Professional obligations.* What are Mason's ethical obligations as a CFA candidate and a member of AIMR?

▧ *Strength of evidence.* Is the evidence sufficient to make an accusation? Mason must act responsibly when making allegations of wrongdoing. His charges must have a basis in fact, and he must ensure that his actions are defensible.

▧ *Expected impact.* What is the probable outcome of reporting the perceived wrongdoing? Are other options available that may be more palatable? Remediation should be a primary goal. So, Mason must consider whether his chosen course of action will result in changes in the firm that will prevent wrongdoing in the future.

▧ *Personal considerations.* Mason must consider how personal considerations are likely to influence his perspective on ethical issues. Should the risk of career-endangering retaliation by the firm take precedence over professional obligations?

Courses of Action. Mason must first determine in his own mind whether legal or ethical violations are occurring. If after further investigation Mason believes Richardson's actions to be unethical (or at least highly suspect), he is faced with another uncomfortable decision. He can (1) do nothing (that is, continue to associate with the perceived unethical activity), (2) pursue the issues internally in hopes of resolution, or (3) resign (completely dissociate from the perceived unethical activity by leaving the firm). As a member of AIMR, Mason cannot take the "do nothing" option. Therefore, he should consider options 2 and 3.

▧ *Confronting Richardson again.* Mason could approach Richardson again, listen to his perspective on the events in question, and provide him with an opportunity to address the perceived problems in an ethically satisfactory way. Richardson may demonstrate to Mason that, contrary to outward appearances, no wrongdoing has occurred. If Richardson admits doing wrong, his actions may be found to be the result more of ignorance than vice or willful neglect, and the problem can be easily corrected.

Mason must make an independent judgment after talking with

Richardson. Does Richardson's explanation make sense? If it does not, should he, knowing that his future with Velstar may be on the line, pursue the issue? Mason's conscience and personal morality, loyalty, and professional obligations are now being put to the test. Consider Mason's option, in the absence of a satisfying response by Richardson, of pursuing the issue with those higher up the chain of command.

▨ *On to Veldine and Page.* If Mason follows this course, he should present his case clearly to Veldine and Page with whatever technical detail and supporting evidence he has mustered. Veldine and Page *should* be supportive of Mason for voicing concern about ethical issues and questionable practices that threaten the firm and its clients.

If in the face of undeniable evidence of wrongdoing, Veldine and Page refuse to address Richardson's conduct, Mason will have to conclude that senior management is not going to be responsive to his concerns and not going to correct the problems. (They may even be complicit in the misconduct.)

At this point, Mason has used all available internal means to address the problem behavior. His immediate supervisor and the firm's principals have had an opportunity to listen and respond; all channels within the firm have been exhausted, to no avail. Mason's problems and their possible consequences now rise to a new level, and his options are severely limited.

▨ *The "R" option.* How can Mason continue to work as if nothing has changed with people he believes are guilty of unethical behavior? How can he hope for success at a firm in which he can put no trust? Is it likely that Richardson, Veldine, and Page will treat Mason as they did prior to these discussions? Neither laws nor compliance guidelines alone can answer such questions. In such a situation, Mason may feel compelled to resign.

Choosing a Course of Action. For a member in a situation such as that in this case, the final choice of actions must be made contextually, not as a matter of general rule. A final ethical decision will come out of the interaction of individual and situational variables. However, although details in "dissenting employee" cases will vary, the recommended process is (1) investigation in order to become reasonably certain of the true situation and then (2) use of internal channels of communications to address the issues directly. The "best case" is for this process to lead to acknowledgment of problems and the development and implementation of preventive guidelines by the firm. In the "worst case," the employee may well conclude that resignation is the only viable alternative.

In the final analysis, whether the behavior of the people in a firm conforms with ethical principles depends on management's ethical beliefs, management's willingness and skills in following through on those beliefs by establishing and implementing compliance policies, and individuals' strength of conviction and perseverance in supporting ethical principles.

Firm Compliance Policies. This case clearly illustrates the necessity for formal compliance guidelines in investment firms. Employees must be allowed to convey their legitimate concerns without fear of retribution. Specific policies could include the following:

- Employees should be required to disclose their knowledge of wrongdoing to appropriate individuals within the organization.
- Communication channels should be established through which employees can make such disclosures in confidence. An open-door policy allowing employees to take their concerns directly to senior managers should be a part of the policy.
- The firm should establish formal procedural guidelines for investigating concerns.
- The firm should guarantee protection for employees who, in good faith, disclose suspected wrongdoing.

Ideally, such policies will encourage employees to report their concerns about possible illegal or unethical activities through designated channels. This approach will, in turn, heighten the sensibilities of employees to potential wrongdoing and help improve the overall ethical climate of the firm.

Preston Partners

Case Facts

Sheldon Preston, CFA, president of Preston Partners, is sitting in his office and pondering the actions he should take in light of the activities of one of his portfolio managers, Gerald Smithson, CFA. As president, Preston has made it a habit to review each day all the Preston Partner trades and the major price changes in the portfolios. Yesterday, he discovered some deeply disturbing information. Several weeks previously, when Preston was on a two-week vacation, Smithson had added to all his clients' portfolios the stock of Utah BioChemical Company, a client of Preston Partners, and of Norgood PLC, a large northern European manufacturer and distributor of drugs and laboratory equipment headquartered in the United Kingdom. Preston had known of a strong, long-standing relationship between Smithson and the president of Utah BioChemical. Indeed, among Smithson's clients were the personal portfolio of Arne Okapuu, president and CEO of Utah BioChemical, and the Utah BioChemical pension fund. Yesterday came the announcement that Utah BioChemical intended to merge with Norgood PLC, and with that news, the share prices of both companies increased more than 40 percent.

The Firm

Preston Partners is a medium-sized investment management firm that specializes in managing large-capitalization portfolios of U.S. equities for pension funds and personal accounts. Preston Partners has adopted the AIMR Code of Ethics and Standards of Professional Conduct as part of the firm's own policy and procedures manual. Preston had written the manual himself but, because he had been pressed for time, had stuck to the key elements rather than addressing all policies in detail. He made sure that every employee received a copy of the manual when he or she joined the firm. Preston thought surely Smithson knew the local securities laws and the Code and Standards even if he hadn't read the manual. Extremely upset, Preston called Smithson into his office for an explanation.

Smithson's Story

While on vacation in London, Smithson narrated, he had seen Okapuu in a restaurant dining with someone he recognized as the chairman of Norgood.

This case was written by Jules A. Huot, CFA, Pension Commission of Ontario.

Their conversation appeared to be intense but very upbeat. Smithson did not attempt to greet Okapuu.

Later, Smithson called on an old analyst friend in London, Andrew Jones, and asked him for some information on Norgood, the stock of which was trading as American Depositary Receipts (ADRs) on the New York Stock Exchange. Jones sent Smithson his firm's latest research report, which was recommending a "hold" on the Norgood stock.

Smithson was already somewhat familiar with the biochemical industry because his large accounts owned other stocks in the industry. Nevertheless, when he returned to the United States, he gathered together several trade journals for background, obtained copies of the two companies' annual reports, and carried out his own due diligence on Utah BioChemical and Norgood.

After thoroughly analyzing both companies' financial history, product lines, and market positions, Smithson concluded that each company's stock was selling at an attractive price based on his valuation. The earnings outlook for Norgood was quite positive, primarily because of the company's presence in the European Union and its strong supplier relationships. Norgood's stock price had shown little volatility but had risen consistently in the past, and the company currently had a strong balance sheet. Utah BioChemical, a leader in the biochemical industry, at one time had been a high-growth stock but had been in a slump in recent years. Based on his analysis of the new products in Utah's pipeline, however, and their market potential, Smithson projected strong sales and cash flow for Utah BioChemical in the future.

Through his research, Smithson also recognized that Utah BioChemical and Norgood were in complementary businesses. Reflecting on what he had seen on his trip to London, Smithson began to wonder if Okapuu was negotiating a merger with or takeover of Norgood.

Convinced of the positive prospects for Utah BioChemical and Norgood, Smithson put in a block trade for 50,000 shares of each company. The purchase orders were executed during the next two weeks.

Smithson had not personally executed a block trade for some time; he usually left execution up to an assistant. Because this trade was so large, however, he decided to handle it himself. He glanced at the section on block trades in Preston Partners' policy and procedures manual, but the discussion was not clear on methods for allocating shares. So, he decided to allocate the shares by beginning with his largest client accounts and working down to the small accounts. Smithson's clients ranged from very conservative personal trust accounts to pension funds with aggressive objectives and guidelines.

At the time of Smithson's decision to make the share purchases, Utah

BioChemical was trading at $10 a share and the Norgood ADRs were trading at $12 a share. During the next two weeks, the price for each company's shares rose several dollars, but no merger or takeover announcement was made—until yesterday.

> *Several activities in this case are or could be violations of the AIMR Code and Standards. Identify possible violations, state what actions Preston and/or Smithson should take to correct the potential violations, and make a short policy statement a firm could use to prevent the violations.*

Case Discussion

Gerald Smithson's story describes some perfectly legitimate actions but also some actions in clear violation of AIMR's Code and Standards. In researching and making the decision to purchase shares of Utah BioChemical and Norgood for his client accounts, Smithson complied with Standard IV(A.1), Reasonable Basis and Representations. He observed a meeting between the heads of two public companies in related businesses, which sparked his interest in researching the companies further. He already had some knowledge of the biochemical industry through some clients' investments and through his relationship with Arne Okapuu, and he carried out his own due diligence on the companies. Smithson had a reasonable basis, supported by appropriate research and investigation, for his investment decision, and he exercised diligence and thoroughness in taking investment action.

Smithson neither possessed nor acted on insider information. He did not actually overhear a conversation; rather, after his research was complete, he "put two and two together" and speculated that the executives might have been discussing a merger or takeover. Viewing the two company leaders together was only one piece of his "mosaic" and was only a small factor in his investment decision-making process. If Smithson had based his decisions solely on his chance viewing of the dinner meeting, the investment decisions would have been inappropriate.

Smithson failed to comply, however, with aspects of the Standards related to the suitability of the investments for his clients and the allocation of trades. In addition, Sheldon Preston failed to exercise his supervisory responsibilities.

Responsibilities to Clients and Interactions with Clients.
Smithson purchased shares in Utah BioChemical Company and Norgood PLC for all of his client portfolios without first determining the suitability or appropriateness of the shares for each account. The case states that the investment objectives and guidelines for Smithson's accounts ranged from conservative, for his personal trust accounts, to aggressive, for his pension

fund clients. Norgood, with its stable stock price, financial strength, and positive earnings outlook, appears to be a conservative stock that would fit within the guidelines of Smithson's more conservative accounts. It may or may not fit the more aggressive guidelines established for some of Smithson's pension fund clients.

Utah BioChemical, however, is probably too volatile to be included in a conservative account and thus may not have been appropriate or suitable for some of the firm's personal trust clients. Therefore, Smithson may have violated Standard IV(B.2), Portfolio Investment Recommendations and Actions, in regard to the appropriateness and suitability of the investment actions he took. Under Standard IV(B.2), an investment manager must consider the client's tolerance for risk, needs, circumstances, goals, and preferences in matching a client with an investment.

Actions required. The case does not make clear whether Smithson's clients have written investment objectives and guideline policy statements. If they do not, Preston should direct Smithson to prepare such written guidelines for all accounts. Smithson should review the guidelines for every account for which he bought shares of Utah BioChemical and Norgood and assess the characteristics of those investments in light of the objectives of the clients and their portfolios. In those accounts for which either investment is unsuitable and inappropriate, he should sell those shares, and Preston Partners should reimburse the accounts for any losses sustained by them.

> *Policy statement for a firm.* "For each client of the firm, portfolio managers, in consultation with the client, shall prepare a written investment policy statement setting out the objectives, the constraints, and the asset-mix policy that meets the needs and circumstances of the client. Managers shall insert this analysis in each client's file. Portfolio managers shall review and confirm the investment policy statements at least annually and whenever the client's business or personal circumstances create a need to review them. In their client relationships, portfolio managers should be alert to any changes in clients' circumstances that would require a policy review.
>
> "When taking investment action, portfolio managers shall consider the appropriateness and suitability of an investment to the needs and circumstances of the client. Managers must satisfy themselves that the basic characteristics of the investment meet the written guidelines for the client's account."

Allocation of Trades. Standard IV(B.3), Fair Dealing, states that members shall deal fairly with clients when taking investment actions. In this case, the firm did not have detailed written guidelines for allocating block trades to client accounts. So, Smithson simply allocated trades to his largest accounts first, at more favorable prices, which discriminated against the smaller accounts. Certain small clients were disadvantaged financially because of Smithson's block-trade allocation method.

Standard IV(B.3) arises out of the investment manager's fiduciary duty and duty of loyalty to clients embodied in the AIMR Code and Standards. Without loyalty, the client cannot trust or rely on the investment manager.

Whenever an investment manager has two or more clients, he or she faces the possibility of showing one client preference over the other. The Code and Standards require that the investment advisor treat each client fairly but do not specify the allocation method to be used. Moreover, treating all clients fairly does not mean that all clients must be treated equally. Equal treatment, given clients' different needs, objectives, and constraints, would be impossible.

Action required. Because Preston Partners has only vague policies for portfolio managers on allocating block trades, Preston needs to formulate detailed guidelines. The trade allocation procedures should be based on guiding principles that ensure (1) fairness to clients, both in priority of execution of orders and in the allocation of the price obtained in the execution of block trades, (2) timeliness and efficiency in the execution of trades, and (3) accuracy in the investment manager's records for trade orders and maintenance of client account positions.

In advance of each trade, portfolio managers should be required to record the account for which the trade is being made and the number of shares being traded.

Block trades are often executed throughout a day or week, which results in many small trades at different prices. To assure that all accounts receive the same average price for each segment of the trade, trades should be allocated to the appropriate accounts just prior to or immediately following each segment of the block trade on a pro rata basis. For example, if 5,000 shares of Norgood and 5,000 shares of Utah BioChemical traded on Day 1, Smithson would have immediately allocated each set of shares to each appropriate account according to the relative size of the account. Each account would thus pay the same average price. If 10,000 more shares traded later that day, or the next day, or so on, Smithson would follow the same procedure.

Preston Partners should disclose procedures for trade allocation to clients in writing at the outset of the client's relationship with the firm. Obtaining full disclosure and the client's consent does not, however, relieve the manager of the responsibility to deal fairly with clients under the Code and Standards.

Policy statement for a firm. "All client accounts participating in a block trade shall receive the same execution price and be charged the same commission, if any. All trade allocations to client accounts shall be made on a pro rata basis prior to or immediately following part or all of a block trade."

Responsibilities of Supervisors. Preston Partners did not have in place supervisory procedures that would have prevented Smithson's allocation approach. Preston's failure to adopt adequate procedures violated Standard III(E), Responsibilities of Supervisors. Preston Partners had adopted the Code and Standards; thus, anyone in the firm with supervisory responsibility should have been thoroughly familiar with the obligation of supervisors under the Code and Standards to assure that proper policies and procedures are in place and are being followed. Supervisors and managers must understand what constitutes an adequate compliance program and must establish proper compliance procedures, preferably designed to prevent rather than simply uncover violations.

The case notes that certain sections of the policy and procedures manual were unclear. Supervisors have a responsibility to assure that compliance policies are clear and well developed. Supervisors and managers must document the procedures and disseminate them to staff. In addition to distributing the policy and procedures manual, they have a responsibility to ensure adequate training of each new employee concerning the key policies and procedures of the firm. Periodic refresher training sessions for all staff are also recommended.

Ultimately, supervisors must take the necessary steps to monitor the actions of all investment professionals and enforce the established policies and procedures.

Actions required. Preston should assure that proper procedures are established that would have prevented the violation committed by Smithson. Preston should assume the responsibility or appoint someone within the firm to become the designated compliance officer whose responsibility is to assure that all policies, procedures, laws, and regulations are being followed by employees.

Policy statement for a firm. "Employees in a supervisory role are responsible for the actions of those under their supervision with regard to compliance with the firm's policies and procedures and any securities laws and regulations that govern employee activities."

Yoshi Investment Counselors (A)

Case Facts

Maggie Fallon, a CFA charterholder and the senior partner at Yoshi Investment Counselors, is reflecting on the past four years of her career. Four years previously, she and three colleagues left the trust department of a large regional bank to form a new investment firm, Yoshi Investment Counselors. She is pleased that the firm has been so successful, with rapid growth in assets, clients, and personnel, but she also knows that Yoshi is at a crossroads. Fallon can see that internal control policies and procedures are necessary to cope with all the changes within the firm, and she believes the firm must implement an effective compliance system.

The Firm. Yoshi Investment Counselors is an investment advisor registered with the U.S. Securities and Exchange Commission. The four founders of Yoshi were successful and experienced portfolio managers, all CFA charterholders, who established the Yoshi partnership to manage equity investments for corporate pension plans on a regional and national basis. Each partner was initially responsible for research coverage of a number of industries and for a single account. Assets under management for the firm's four accounts totaled $54 million. In addition to the four partners, Yoshi employed a trader, a quantitative analyst, and a secretary. The firm had no separate marketing or compliance staff.

The First Six Months. During a meeting held shortly after Yoshi's formation, one of the partners raised the issue of whether the firm should do anything about instituting a system of compliance with legal, ethical, and professional responsibilities. Another partner replied, "I'm not sure whether we need a formal compliance program, given our limited staff and scale of operations. Besides," he continued, "we all know what and what not to do; we all hold CFA charters, we've read AIMR's Code of Ethics and Standards of Professional Conduct, and we all sign AIMR's Professional Conduct Statement each year."

Fallon commented, "I would like to see us not only establish compliance guidelines but also develop a strong ethical culture in the firm. It goes beyond 'keeping our noses clean.' The issue isn't so much whether we need a formal compliance program but how we can develop and

This case was written by Douglas R. Hughes, CFA.

implement an *effective* program and what our primary goal for the program should be. It seems to me that in our business, the opportunities for individuals and firms to behave unethically or illegally are almost limitless. All of us need to maintain a high degree of ethical awareness and promote an environment in the firm that is conducive to ethical behavior. I believe a good compliance program makes sense for reasons beyond simply keeping us out of jail.

"Having said that, let me also remind you that quarterly results are the name of the game, and when all is said and done, we're in the investment business to earn a good living: If the firm does well, you will personally benefit. As you know, we put a lot of thought into structuring a compensation program that gives us all the incentive to increase assets and profitability. So, let's also keep our bottom line in mind."

As the first six months progressed, Fallon continued from time to time to have some concerns about ethics and compliance. "What are the danger signs that a firm like ours is at risk?" she wondered. "Are we overlooking potential ethical or legal problems because of operational, marketing, personnel, or maybe most significantly for us, financial considerations? What should my own role be? What can we do to keep the firm properly anchored, ethically speaking? Should I add a compliance officer to the staff or give an existing staff member compliance responsibilities?"

As a CFA charterholder, Fallon knew that these considerations were important, but she always concluded that the best use of her time right now was picking stocks and putting more business on the books to enhance the profitability of the firm. She believed that new business could skyrocket if Yoshi achieved the kind of performance she was confident, given the exceptional investment talent, it could achieve.

Three Years of Rapid Growth. During the next three years, Yoshi Investment Counselors experienced excellent investment performance. With new accounts added during this period, assets under management grew to $1.3 billion. The staff also increased through the addition of four portfolio managers, another trader, a marketing specialist, three research assistants, and two secretaries.

The firm's growth introduced some problems, however—with respect not only to managing the business but also to compliance. Administrative and managerial problems have been cropping up with increasing frequency. Breakdowns are beginning to surface in trading and record keeping. Rapid account growth has reduced the effectiveness of client service. Client communication is beginning to deteriorate because the partners and other portfolio managers are carrying excessive account loads. Problems are also developing with respect to adherence to client guidelines and constraints, and internal reviews of client accounts are becoming slipshod.

Recognizing that the firm may be in the early stages of losing its performance momentum, effectiveness with clients, and internal control, Fallon calls a partners meeting. She begins by saying, "We are in danger of being victimized by our own success. Let's reassess where we are. Are we emphasizing growth and profitability to the detriment of our client base? Are we putting ourselves at risk from the standpoint of compliance and ethical conduct? What more could we be doing to instill a sense of concern for clients and professional responsibility within Yoshi?"

> *Discuss why a firm should implement a compliance program during its start-up phase. As a firm goes through a period of rapid growth, what are the potential dangers that can indicate that a firm is at legal or ethical risk? Outline for Fallon the objectives and essential elements of an effective compliance program and the role of the AIMR Code and Standards in that program. What actions should Fallon take to improve or correct the current situation?*

Case Discussion

The partners of Yoshi Investment Counselors recognize the importance of compliance policies and procedures, but the realities of daily life and the desire to achieve the firm's financial goals, as well as the partners' personal financial goals, have intervened between their ideals and their behavior.

Reasons for a Formal Compliance System. The primary reason for an investment management firm to establish a formal compliance system is to prevent unethical or illegal actions. Such actions can be costly—not only to individuals but also to the firm. Unethical or illegal actions by even one individual can damage or destroy an otherwise reputable and successful organization.

Although ultimate responsibility for ethical actions rests with individuals, the firm has the ability and obligation to establish a corporate culture that promotes ethical conduct. Exclusive emphasis on individual behavior ignores the importance of a firm's ability to shape and guide that behavior. Individuals are governed by their own internal rules and values; the combination of personal values and the firm's values yields decisions that may be significantly different from those based on personal knowledge or values alone. By promoting proper conduct and professionalism within its ranks, the firm makes clear that individual responsibility goes hand in hand with accountability to the firm.

Additional reasons why Yoshi should implement an effective compliance program are as follows:

■ *To meet legal requirements.* A formal compliance program is the most effective way for a firm to meet its legal requirements to supervise its employees. A well-conceived, well-implemented program can prevent or significantly limit violations, thereby reducing the likelihood of legal, regulatory, or professional sanctions. In addition, such a program can serve as an affirmative defense for the firm if legal action is taken against it.

▨ *To avoid public embarrassment.* By deterring employee misconduct, compliance guidelines reduce the likelihood of violations that could result in adverse publicity and public embarrassment.

▨ *To provide guidance on complex issues.* Questions of personal and organizational accountability and liability in all spheres of investing are vastly more complex and pervasive today than they were only a few years ago. Compliance guidelines can minimize the burden of complex regulations by doing what they are intended to do—provide guidance.

▨ *To maintain a competitive edge.* Recognition is growing that corporate culture can be nurtured and that corporate ethics can add a competitive edge to a firm's performance. A firm may have no better marketing tool than to have a reputation for personal integrity combined with investment competence.

All investment firms need to ensure that their employees know how to deal with ethical issues in their everyday work lives. When the ethical climate is clear and positive, all employees will know what is expected of them and can act with the understanding that what they are doing is proper and is supported by top management and other members of the firm.

Actions required. The partners of Yoshi Investment Counselors need to make a serious commitment to ethics and professional responsibility. The stakes are too high for not taking ethics seriously.

Danger Signs. Yoshi has enjoyed rapid growth and good performance, but as a result, certain areas that are closely related to the management of client accounts are suffering. Several danger signs could alert Yoshi that it is at ethical or legal risk:

▨ *Unyielding emphasis on the bottom line.* Yoshi has emphasized growth of assets under management to the detriment of existing clients, and although Fallon is at least considering compliance issues, the bottom line remains uppermost in her mind. When firms believe that financial success is the only criterion worthy of consideration and that high standards of conduct are obstacles or impediments to such success, their attention is focused too heavily on the bottom line. The danger is that a firm will be unwilling to take an ethical stand when such action has a financial cost.

▨ *Emphasis on the short term.* Fallon says that "quarterly results are the name of the game." When a firm's emphasis is on the short term—for example, short-term investment performance—pressure may be put on employees to make decisions that are not in the best interests of their clients.

▧ *Compensation programs that create undue pressure on employees.* Special compensation or other incentive arrangements can have a significant effect on an investment manager's objectivity. Such programs can create a potential conflict of interest between doing what is right and doing what is necessary to improve personal performance.

▧ *Lack of a senior-level compliance officer.* Every investment firm, large or small, should have a designated compliance officer with oversight responsibilities. This individual plays a vital role as the firm takes steps to shape the conduct of its employees.

Actions required. Yoshi should address the potential danger areas by clearly stating that the firm believes that ethics and profits are not mutually exclusive, either in principle or in practice. Similarly, Yoshi should avoid incentive compensation programs that create pressure to achieve short-term performance goals that may be contrary to client objectives or that result in preferential treatment to certain clients. At a minimum, special compensation arrangements should be fully disclosed to clients.

An Effective Compliance System. An effective compliance system will help Fallon manage the firm in all stages of its growth. The sooner a compliance program is in place, even for a start-up firm, the less likely that the firm will be faced with compliance problems. The key elements of a program or system for ensuring ethical and legal compliance include making client interests the central goal of the firm, incorporating well-thought-out guidelines, obtaining a commitment from senior management, designating a compliance officer, implementing employee training, and enforcing the program.

▧ *Client-centered goals.* Because the investment profession affects the financial well-being of individuals who depend on its services, the investing public has every right to evaluate professional services from an ethical as well as a technical perspective. During the past 10 years, however, wrongdoing in the investment industry, arising from bad judgment and widely reported in the media, has heightened public skepticism about the profession.

To overcome the public's adverse perceptions, whether real or imagined, investment managers must establish trust between themselves and their clients. Client opinions about an investment manager's trustworthiness and personal integrity can overshadow all other values the firm may be trying to represent. The trust of clients can be gained by putting clients' interests first and by subordinating personal interests and those of the firm.

    ▓ *Incorporating guidelines: AIMR's Code and Standards.* Upon enrolling in the CFA Program or becoming AIMR members, individuals commit themselves to a philosophy grounded in the Code of Ethics and Standards of Professional Conduct. The Code and Standards describe the general value system of AIMR and provide guidelines for making decisions that are consistent with those principles. Although knowledge of ethical standards alone does not ensure that an individual will adhere to those standards, such knowledge is a requisite part of the professional competence expected of all CFA candidates, CFA charterholders, and other AIMR members.

The AIMR Standards are intended to be the cornerstone in the relationships between members and the organization and between individual members and their clients. In this way, they serve the members and the profession by building public trust.

    ▓ *Role of senior management.* The ethical climate of an organization is set at the top. The culture that top management establishes and reinforces plays a significant part in the way employees view the importance of ethics within the firm. The leadership of top management gives life to an ethics agenda. In fact, the posture of top management may be the single most important factor in determining ethical behavior in an organization.

    ▓ *Using a compliance system to manage the growth of the firm.* Most investment decisions have ethical ramifications whether investment professionals realize it or not. When the actions taken are proper, the ethical dimension goes unnoticed and attention is focused on the astuteness of the decisions. When actions go astray, the firm realizes, too late, its mistake in ignoring ethical guidelines.

The imperatives of day-to-day organizational performance are often so compelling that a firm has little time or inclination to give attention to the ethical dimension of decision making. Rules, procedures, and other control mechanisms often lag the growth of a firm, creating opportunities for employees to behave unethically because no up-to-date rules prescribe behavior.

Yoshi finds itself in this position. Management should have attempted to control growth—and its manifest problems—rather than be controlled by it. Unfortunately, problems concerning the servicing of client accounts have already occurred. If "internal reviews of client accounts are becoming slipshod," growth has clearly overtaken the firm's compliance capabilities and the firm is vulnerable to events of a preventable nature. Fallon is correct in noting that the time is overdue to assess the level of ethical awareness and policy effectiveness at Yoshi.

▨ *Compliance officer.* A specifically designated compliance officer is an essential element of an effective compliance program. A compliance officer is someone who has the responsibility, ability, or authority to affect behavior and respond to misconduct. This individual should hold a central position in the firm and be fully integrated in the management and decision-making process. In order to be in a position to advise the firm's employees, the compliance officer should be informed regarding laws, proposed legislation, government regulations, and current industry conditions.

▨ *Training.* Investment firms have a responsibility to contribute in any way they can to the ethical development of their employees. Preparing a compliance manual and providing training in ethical decision making can help employees understand that ethical questions are integral to their daily experience. If the training is effective, it will help employees be alert in perceiving ethical issues, be aware of the reasons underlying the ethical principles, and be equipped to reason carefully in applying the principles in the investment decision-making process.

▨ *Enforcement.* Employees are required to comply with both the letter and the spirit of compliance guidelines, of course, but clients and the public can be protected and the integrity of the guidelines can be maintained only if the guidelines are strictly enforced. In turn, effective enforcement can be achieved only if violations are brought to the attention of senior management and promptly resolved.

Actions required. Yoshi needs to determine what its ethical risks are in the normal course of business and then provide guidance in those areas. Yoshi must articulate and communicate ethical principles, whether based on AIMR Standards or on the firm's own design, and inculcate them in the culture of the firm. These standards become obligations of Yoshi staff as a result of their employment and serve as a guide for behavior.

Fallon should take steps now to implement an effective compliance program in line with the points outlined in this discussion. The best insurance Yoshi could have against the loss of trust is adherence to the highest standards of ethical and professional conduct. The first step in the process would be to define client interests as the firm's number one priority. Yoshi should continue with the development of a policy specifying ethical objectives and providing formal guidelines for ethical behavior. Then, Yoshi should develop a compliance program to serve as a mechanism for holding employees accountable to this goal. Compliance guidelines have no meaning unless effectively implemented. With a solid compliance program in place, the firm can focus on the specific investment objectives and constraints of each individual client. The policy should make clear that this process continues through periodic reviews to determine whether changes in client circumstances require revisions in investment policy.

Yoshi should designate a current senior-level staff member as a compliance officer or (if no one is suitable in this rapidly growing firm) should hire a compliance officer responsible for overseeing the firm's ethics and for steering the firm around legal and ethical pitfalls.

Yoshi should encourage ethical behavior by conducting regular training sessions for new employees and by informing all employees about changes in applicable laws, regulations, and other compliance requirements.

Fallon should use her position to promote the ethical consciousness of the firm by emphasizing that ethical behavior is important and expected. She must be openly and strongly committed to ethical conduct and provide constant leadership in tending to and renewing the values of the organization; she must exemplify the guiding principles in her day-to-day activities; and she must evaluate the performance of others in view of those principles. Fallon needs to communicate to employees that their failure to behave in accordance with an established compliance program will generate significant personal and firm costs and that any individual who violates the rules will be subject to disciplinary action. In addition, although the principal purpose of enforcement should be to encourage compliance rather than to administer punishment, the credible threat of punishment would provide leverage in Yoshi's attempt to maintain the firm's integrity and well-being.

In summary, Fallon can institute a formal and effective compliance program at Yoshi by ensuring that the program

- has her full support and that of the other partners,
- reflects the nature of the firm (based on size, services offered, and complexity of products, for example),
- is understandable to all employees,
- meets, and preferably exceeds, minimum industry standards,
- is continually reviewed and revised to ensure it remains up-to-date,
- includes an individual with compliance responsibilities,
- is communicated to employees, including regular education and training, and
- includes enforcement procedures.

Yoshi Investment Counselors (B)

Case Facts

Yoshi Investment Counselors' performance numbers remain strong as the firm enters its fifth year of operation, and account growth continues unabated. In the previous year, Yoshi implemented a compliance program consisting of three elements. First is a code of ethics, which includes broad principles emphasizing Yoshi's commitment to an ethical workplace. Yoshi also uses AIMR's *Standards of Practice Handbook*, which provides a basic ethical framework, set forth in the Code of Ethics, and offers specific guidelines for investment managers in the Standards of Professional Conduct, the accompanying commentary, and the topical studies. The second element of the program is Yoshi's designation of a compliance officer to monitor employees and keep abreast of legal and regulatory changes. Jeb Wilson, CFA, one of Yoshi's founding partners, has become responsible for compliance through his appointment to be Yoshi's chief operating officer. The third element of the compliance program is procedures to enforce the code that include disciplinary sanctions—from verbal reprimand to letter of censure, reduction in merit pay or bonus, and dismissal.

Toward the end of the first four years, the partners also made a major strategic decision to expand management capabilities into fixed-income securities and foreign equities. This change has required staff additions— five portfolio managers, eight analysts, two marketing assistants, another trader, five research assistants, and four secretaries. When the hiring is complete, Yoshi's employee count will be 43.

Before the hiring is finished, Senior Partner Maggie Fallon, CFA, meets with Wilson one afternoon to discuss a matter that has been on her mind since the decision was made to increase the size of Yoshi. Fallon explains to Wilson, "Jeb, with our firm's personnel expansion nearly complete, I'd like you to devise an ethics and compliance training program. I don't see our present system of simply sending around copies of new regulatory pronouncements as particularly effective or stimulating to our employees. The program would initially focus on the new employees, but I'd like to integrate the rest of us into it very soon and continue training everybody on an ongoing basis."

This case was written by Douglas R. Hughes, CFA.

"I hope we can avoid a blasé attitude toward training," Fallon continues. "I realize training is not on the top of everyone's 'to do' list, but we're taking too many risks if we ignore it. Also, as you know, I think a strong ethical 'corporate culture' is important to us and our clients, and training will contribute to getting that culture. With the dramatic increase in our staff, it's an important time for us—a great opportunity, it seems to me, to instill an ethical culture and set up a training program.

"Jeb, I'd like you to come up with some realistic training goals for Yoshi and describe the steps that we could take to accomplish those goals. In addition, I'd like your thoughts on what we should expect of our training efforts within the overall context of compliance in the firm. Should we be doing more? If so, what?"

> *Discuss appropriate training goals and specific components of an effective training program for Yoshi. Also discuss the role of training within a comprehensive compliance program.*

Case Discussion

Jeb Wilson needs to consider a number of issues. Primary among them are the goals of Yoshi's training program and the steps to take and factors to consider in developing the program. In addition, Wilson must respond to Maggie Fallon's request for ideas on the role of training within Yoshi's overall compliance and ethics efforts.

Training Goals. Fallon wants training to be an integral and complementary component of change and growth within the firm. If Yoshi is like most investment firms, the vast majority of its employees strive to act in a professional, ethical manner. They may not always have the appropriate knowledge or awareness of ethical issues, however, to ensure consistent ethical conduct; the ethical dimension of investment-related issues and situations is sometimes difficult to discern. An obvious goal of ethics training, then, is to teach employees, first, how to develop an awareness of ethical problems or dilemmas that they may confront and, second, how to apply ethical skills and reasoning in the decision-making process.

Yoshi has demonstrated considerable investment expertise in four years. The linking of technical competence and ethical competence should be a major goal of the training program. Yoshi's employees should understand more than the rudiments of ethical behavior. Ethical competence should, in turn, promote proper conduct as employees link their behavior to their ethical reasoning. Wilson should understand that, although training cannot guarantee a reduction in ethical violations, it can go a long way toward making ethics a factor to be considered in the investment management process and can provide the employees with a basis for ethical reasoning. Successful training is particularly important in today's world of changes in public attitudes and values, increased legal and governmental influences, and changes within the investment business itself (in terms of both size and complexity).

By implementing a training program, Yoshi can clearly demonstrate its commitment to ethical behavior and an ethically oriented culture. An effective training program reassures employees that ethical standards and conduct will be supported and rewarded by the organization. Therefore, training can play a major role in making employees aware of their individual ethical responsibilities.

Fallon has recognized that learning from mistakes is not an attractive option in the investment business. Proper ethical and compliance training can have wide-ranging beneficial repercussions for the organization if the training improves ethical behavior and prevents mistakes from happening.

Steps in Developing a Program. Steps to take in developing and implementing a formal training program include analyzing employee and manager needs, choosing/developing curriculum and training methods, obtaining feedback on the program, and program evaluation.

Laying the groundwork: Needs analysis. Wilson first must determine what kinds of ethical problems Yoshi's employees have or are likely to have. What are the key ethical issues facing specific individuals or the organization as a whole? Is a widespread pattern of ethical problems apparent, or do ethical issues relate largely to isolated cases?

Wilson's analysis should include examination of organizational processes and pressures. Is anything impinging on the employees' range of ethical choices? To the extent that an ethical problem exists, is it because employees do not know a violation exists, do not know how to respond, or do not want to respond? Is Yoshi prepared to deal with any problems that exist? Do certain areas need special emphasis because of regulatory actions, new regulations, or new laws? In answering these questions, Wilson will begin to see specific needs surface, and the ethics training program can start to take shape.

Wilson should also consider assembling an in-house focus group to discuss ethics and compliance training. Employees can and should play an active part in setting training goals. He should seek full cooperation and support of senior and lower-level employees in all functional areas in developing topics for emphasis.

Curriculum and training methods. A firm's training program should take into account the existing level of ethics knowledge among employees and balance the needs of the firm against constraints in time, money, and other resources. Accordingly, a critical aspect of training is that each element have a purpose; if a particular subject is taught, the employees should understand the reason.

Wilson's groundwork should dictate the content of the training program—the specific ethical knowledge and skills the employees need to perform their jobs properly. The next step is to organize instructional materials into a curriculum that supports the learning objectives. In a program for new employees, the curriculum may need to include basic ethical and compliance topics; ongoing programs must be able to integrate the latest information on rules, regulations, and laws and their implications for various job functions.

Wilson also should establish processes for distributing relevant literature, and reference materials should be accessible to all employees. A particularly useful addition to the usual required readings and lectures in a formal training program is case studies and analyses. The case method allows employees to become part of various decision-making situations that involve ethical dilemmas. By transporting employees into realistic situations, interactions, and unresolved dilemmas, the case method requires them to select a course of action using the knowledge and skills they accumulate through the training program. The cases should obviously include situations and scenarios that Yoshi employees are likely to encounter.

Yoshi might also wish to avail itself of computer technology and software that allow interactive training within the firm or by accessing relevant information from outside sources, such as regulatory agencies.

Training sessions should be scheduled regularly, and these regular sessions should be supplemented as needed in response to changing circumstances in the firm or the industry.

▨ *Feedback and evaluation.* Feedback on training programs is essential to ensure that the organization's training goals are being met and that training is being focused in the right directions. Initial and ongoing employee evaluations will help Wilson determine what training areas should be continued, what should be enhanced, and what should be curtailed or totally eliminated.

Wilson also needs to carry out his own evaluation of the program's performance. Are Yoshi's employees more alert in perceiving ethical issues after training than before, more aware of the reasons underlying the ethical principles, more equipped to reason carefully in applying the principles to the specific situations they encounter? Is employee behavior being favorably affected? Is the firm avoiding significant ethical problems?

Additional Components of the Compliance Program. Training is a key to increasing ethical awareness and knowledge of what actions to take in ethical dilemmas, but training is only one component of the firm's overall system for promoting compliance and ethical conduct. Other important aspects are as follows:

▨ *Employee selection.* Yoshi should hire only those individuals whose values and beliefs are consistent with an ethically responsible culture.

▨ *Top-management support.* Fallon and the other senior managers should encourage ethical consciousness within Yoshi by serving as examples, by demonstrating consistency between ethical principles and ethical behavior, and by reinforcing the ethical culture.

▨ *Reinforcement of ethical commitment.* Employees should be required to read and affirm the principles embodied in the firm's code and standards by signing a document to that effect annually.

▨ *Reinforcement of ethical behavior.* Firms reinforce ethical behavior primarily by encouraging compliance with established standards rather than administering punishment, but the standards of desired ethical behavior must be backed up with specific procedures for enforcement, for handling unethical conduct. Carrying out this mandate is not as simple as it may seem; the firm must define and understand what constitutes ethical versus unethical behavior, develop a system to monitor and report ethical/ unethical behavior, and develop a performance appraisal system that includes ethical criteria.

▨ *Ethics committee.* Yoshi has designated a compliance officer, but the firm might benefit from a corporate ethics committee to monitor and investigate compliance, clarify policy-related issues, serve as a final authority on the policy's meaning, recommend changes in policy, and receive reports of suspicious or unethical behavior.

▨ *Policy review.* Ethics policies should be reviewed periodically—at a minimum, annually.

▨ *Personnel reviews.* Ethical decision making should be integrated into the performance appraisal process.

Yoshi Investment Counselors (C)

Case Facts

Jeb Wilson, CFA, chief operating officer and head of compliance, is well acquainted with Yoshi Investment Counselors' operations and is becoming knowledgeable about the compliance area, but training, particularly developing and implementing a formal program, is a completely new endeavor for him. "Where do I begin?" he wonders.

He decides that a good starting point will be to identify specific problem areas where training may be needed and determine employee attitudes toward training. He brings together a group of employees representing a cross-section of the firm for a give-and-take session on ethics and compliance training.

During the two-hour meeting, he receives many suggestions and words of encouragement. Some of the comments are troubling, however, and he has difficulty responding adequately to them in the meeting. For example, Larry Evans, a newly hired fixed-income manager, says, "Jeb, I appreciate what you're saying about the need for a formal training program, but to be quite candid, I think I'm perfectly capable of dealing with ethical dilemmas without time-consuming training sessions. Ethical behavior is just a matter of letting yourself be governed by your own internal laws and values, doing what you think is right. What could be simpler? Acceptable behavior is self-evident; we don't need to be schooled in it."

Kathy Knight, a senior portfolio manager, agrees: "Do I believe in the importance of ethics? Of course I do, but a training program to teach good ethics? Come on! I mean, can good character and ethical judgment really be taught? My attitudes were developed long ago, well before I entered the investment profession. My moral compass is set, and I think I'm pointed in the right direction without the need for sermonizing on the job."

"Ethics is such a personal matter, and it's so situation specific," adds one of the newly hired equity analysts, Gina Jackson. "To come up with hard-and-fast rules for dealing with specific types of ethical problems seems fruitless. It seems to me that each problem must be dealt with individually and within its own context. How can we apply general ethical principles, such as our code, to specific dilemmas and decisions arising in our professional practice? Besides, many ethical issues lie in a grey

---

This case was written by Douglas R. Hughes, CFA.

zone where clear-cut right or wrong answers may not even exist. We all know the diversity of activities and the range of potential problems in the investment management business. All of these things make it extremely difficult to arrive at *the* answer when confronted by an ethical dilemma."

Tinh Liu, the newly hired trader, comments, "Jeb, I'm a trader. I don't do marketing presentations. I don't even see our clients. I execute orders. Why do I need to waste my time learning about performance presentation or the basis on which investment recommendations should be made or anything else outside my immediate area of responsibility?"

"I know as a firm we have a reputation to uphold, but isn't knowledge and obedience of the law sufficient? Can't we cover our bases by simply acting legally?" asks Tracy Simms, a newly hired marketing assistant. "Just tell me what the laws and regulations are, keep me updated, and I'll be satisfied. That's really all I need."

Lance Albritton, a senior portfolio manager and long-term employee, adds, "It seems to me that 'ethics' doesn't really add to the firm's bottom line. And as for training, it takes time and other resources away from our primary function of money management. Is all this concern necessary, especially if our actions, as Tracy mentioned, are within the bounds of legality?"

> *What are some of the errors or misconceptions in the thinking of these employees? Put yourself in the place of Jeb Wilson and consider how you could respond to such comments.*

Case Discussion

The employee comments in this case raise issues related to the usefulness and cost of programs for training in ethics and compliance, the need for specificity in the firm's ethical guidelines, cross-training, and the sufficiency of compliance with laws and regulations.

Training's Usefulness. The comments made by Larry Evans and Kathy Knight show deep skepticism about the effectiveness of ethics training. Many factors go into making an ethical decision, including one's own "internal laws and values," but training can also have a meaningful impact. At a minimum, training will alert employees to the issues, teach reasoning skills, assist employees in dealing effectively with ethical challenges, and create a supportive ethical environment for employees. Employees can be made sensitive to ethics through effective training.

The Need for Specificity. Gina Jackson made a valid point. Ethical decision making is, in fact, to a great extent determined by situation; specific circumstances make a difference in terms of appropriate ethical response, and as a result, the application of general principles may not provide much assistance in resolving specific ethical dilemmas. Nevertheless, although each situation must be dealt with individually, Jackson needs to understand that the resolution of a situation can be based on the values she holds individually *and* on the expectations the firm has for her. No training program can specify what to do in every situation, but training can present employees with a range of circumstances that they are likely to encounter and provide a prescribed way to handle them. If a code of ethics and compliance program are explicitly stated and presented to employees in training sessions, unethical actions are less likely to occur and are less deniable if they do occur.

With respect to Jackson's comment about the difficulty in arriving at "*the* answer" when confronted with an ethical dilemma, it is important for Wilson to point out that ethics training should allow her to select, not necessarily the best or most effective action, but a course of action that is appropriate and acceptable to her and the firm.

Cross-Training. Tinh Liu questioned the need to be involved in training that seemingly will not affect him. On the surface, his concerns make sense, but other factors should be addressed before Yoshi decides to segregate training on a strict functional basis.

First, much of the training Yoshi will eventually conduct is likely to be "generic." All Yoshi employees are expected to practice within the ethical boundaries of the firm, and all are expected to adhere to the firm's policies and to meet professional standards, which are firmwide in nature, not function specific. Liu, like all employees, has an obligation to maintain and promote the welfare of the firm; his allegiance should be to the policies and practices of the firm as a whole. Broad-based training can play an important role in this regard.

A second factor that supports the need for some integration in training is the interaction that takes place in an investment organization, particularly a small or medium-size firm like Yoshi. Employees do not work in a vacuum. Investment decision making and actions require considerable coordination and integration. Even though Liu has a separate job, his actions affect other employees and the firm itself. Each employee is a critical link in the firm's total ethical environment.

A third basis for ethics cross-training is the contribution it can make to a system of internal control. Ethical problems can arise in many areas of the investment process, and broad-based training will sensitize employees to the ethical issues faced by coworkers and enable them to grasp the seriousness and complexity of those issues. The result can be a shared sense of responsibility for upholding the group's ethical obligations. Cross-training also has implications for detecting and reporting aberrant behavior by others.

Compliance with the Law: Good Enough? The fallacy of Tracy Simms's comments lies in the fact that ethics is not simply a matter of complying with existing laws and regulations; ethical compliance represents a higher standard that goes beyond legal compliance. A profession that places its practitioners in a fiduciary capacity in managing others' funds must set a higher level of responsibility than the law. (In the investment industry, ethical issues often serve as precursors to changes in laws and regulations.)

Professionalism also plays a role. In addition to the expectation that a professional will possess certain specialized knowledge and technical skills, professional competence extends to professional integrity. Adherence to ethical standards going beyond that which is mandated by law is a key element in one's identity as a professional.

The Cost of Ethics. Lance Albritton was correct in asserting that a firmwide commitment to integrating ethics into the decision-making process through a formal training program may entail financial costs. Compliance programs have costs in the form of time and resources. Some organizations may even gain short-term benefits from unethical actions— for example, a firm acquiring clients by overstating its investment performance or by paying rebates to secure business. So, ethics and ethics training may not affect the bottom line positively and may even detract from the bottom line in the short term. In the long run, however, a firm cannot operate if its prevailing culture is inconsistent with that of its clients and the profession as a whole. By taking ethics seriously, Yoshi is recognizing that its reputation is a valuable asset, one whose value the firm hopes to preserve.

Moreover, an ethical culture is likely to have a positive impact on the quality of the work environment and in the way the firm deals not only with clients and others outside the firm but also with employees. Ethical behavior may increase the morale and motivation among employees and attract high-quality people who enjoy working for a respected firm. A firm perceived as unethical suffers from the lack of respect and trust among employees and existing or prospective clients.

Yoshi Investment Counselors (D)

Case Facts

Upon completion of Yoshi Investment Counselors' recent hiring activities, Senior Partner Maggie Fallon, CFA, decides to welcome the new employees formally at an orientation meeting. Following are excerpts from her speech:

"What has made our firm thrive, both in terms of economics and job satisfaction, is a special glue composed of many constituent parts: technical competence, mutual respect for each other's strengths and abilities, commitment to share one's knowledge and experience, belief in the continuing importance of personal integrity, and (and this last point is very important because it brings everything together) a strong ethical culture. These factors have given us a competitive edge in attracting and keeping the talent we need to succeed.

"We are now in the process of setting new and higher goals for performance excellence, growth, and broader client services that will take us to the end of this decade and beyond. We must achieve our goals without compromising the integrity and ethical commitment that have been a mainstay of our firm.

"We all know that sound investment practice requires the assessment of all relevant information in reaching an investment decision. Examining the ethical implications of the actions and decisions should be a critical component in the entire process. I believe good ethics is good business. We must hold each other accountable in the conduct of our day-to-day activities. One person can sink a ship, and a company, just like an individual, can destroy itself through arrogance and inattention.

"Although ultimate responsibility for your actions rests with you as individuals, promoting ethical conduct is not a strictly individual endeavor. The firm has an obligation too, and here again, corporate culture comes into the picture. It is the key ingredient.

"After we wrap up this orientation meeting, I'd like you to think about three questions. First, why do people act ethically? Second, what causes people to act unethically in a business setting? Finally, what can we, as a firm, do to guide or promote ethical decision making?"

This case was written by Douglas R. Hughes, CFA.

> *Discuss the importance of Fallon's comments to the new employees in the orientation meeting. Respond to Fallon's questions concerning the factors that cause employees to behave ethically or unethically in a business situation.*

Case Discussion

Fallon's comments are significant in two important ways—as a demonstration of top management's resolve to promote ethical behavior and as a communication of expectations to employees at their time of entry into the firm. In ethics, top management's role is central; in fact, the attitudes and actions of senior managers may be the single most important factor in fostering a climate of high ethical standards within a firm—because top management is in a unique position to raise and maintain standards of conduct and to set a tone that permeates the entire organization. If senior managers do not support ethical conduct, subordinates are less likely to behave ethically.

A company's ethical philosophy must be made explicit and must be supported by the firm's leadership. Accordingly, Fallon is demonstrating her willingness to contribute to the ethical development of Yoshi's employees by implementing and communicating policies that do not tolerate unethical behavior.

Orientation of New Employees. Fallon's decision to emphasize ethical concerns in an orientation speech shows that she recognizes that, even though enhancing organizational commitment to ethical behavior is an ongoing process, gaining commitment is critical early in an employee's association with the firm. Research has shown that commitment to the organization is a major factor in predicting ethical behavior. Individuals who are committed to an organization's ethical policies early in their employment are more likely to remain committed throughout their tenure with the organization. Thus, firms must have mechanisms to enhance commitment to the firm during the early stages of employment.

For employees to be part of a strong ethical culture, they must be educated about the expectations and practices of the organization, which is exactly the approach Fallon was taking in this speech and Yoshi is taking in the training program. Part of the orientation should include a requirement that new employees read and sign a statement obligating them to comply with the firm's ethical standards.

The employees' decisions to join Yoshi should have been predicated, in part, on an appreciation of the firm's ethical foundation and its core values. If their personal beliefs were not congruent with Yoshi's organizational objectives, prospective employees should have looked elsewhere for employment. Similarly, the firm, if it recognized the incongruity, should not have extended an employment offer.

Influences on Behavior. Fallon's questions at the end of her speech are a further effort to sensitize Yoshi employees to the importance of ethics in the firm. In answer to Fallon's first question, a number of influences—often interacting—can be noted that promote ethical decision making:

▨ *Individual characteristics.* Personal factors that influence an individual's ethical system include knowledge, values, beliefs, attitudes, personality, conscience, background, and concern about the likely consequences of unethical actions. A firm can address these factors in its employment policies by hiring individuals with not only technical competence but also a strong sense of ethics.

▨ *Organizational practices and corporate culture.* The organization can exert a powerful influence on the behavior of its members through training, corporate guidelines, and reinforcement of desired behavior.

▨ *Supervisors and coworkers.* Individuals often model their behavior on the behavior of people they perceive to be important. In a business setting, the models are usually people in senior positions. The attitudes and actions of top managers and immediate supervisors, therefore, are a critical influence on the ethical behavior of employees. Fallon and the other senior managers are important models in the organizational lives of Yoshi employees.

A number of factors are also significant in causing people to act unethically. Often the *source* of influence is the same for ethical and unethical behavior; it is the characteristics of the source that promote the opposite effects:

▨ *Predisposition and personal self-interest.* Certain individuals may have an inclination toward unethical behavior; personality may play a role. The perceived trade-off between expected penalties and expected personal gains may favor unethical acts, and certain organizations or functions may provide more opportunities for unethical actions than others.

▨ *Pressure.* Superiors—immediate supervisors or senior managers—may place pressures on individuals to behave unethically. Such pressures may be subtle; for example, the imperatives of day-to-day performance may encourage striving for the most profitable or economically expedient solution regardless of whether it is ethical.

▨ *Behavior of coworkers.* Peer pressure may lead an individual to unethical behavior, even if such behavior goes against the individual's own attitudes. A belief that "everyone else is doing it" leads to "it's okay for me to do it."

▨ *Lack of knowledge.* The inability to recognize ethical issues can result in unethical behavior. Employees must know what is correct behavior and what is not.

▓ *Absence of a corporate ethics policy.* A contributor to lack of knowledge is the absence of corporate policies. Lack of policies also affects the organization's culture. An organizational culture that is not clear and positive can predispose members to behave unethically.

▓ *Lack of professional guidelines or standards of behavior.* Another contributor to lack of knowledge is the absence of professional standards, which provide principles and guidelines for ethical actions.

Yoshi Investment Counselors (E)

Case Facts

On the day after the orientation session conducted by Senior Partner Maggie Fallon, CFA, three of the new employees, Jane Sondheim, Ray DeFario, and Anthony Glynn, make an appointment to see Chief Operating Officer Jeb Wilson, CFA, to reflect on Fallon's comments and to raise a few questions.

Sondheim begins, "I was impressed with Maggie's comments yesterday, but I want to ask you about a few things. First, on corporate culture. Everyone talks about it; Maggie said a strong corporate culture was critical. But what is it? My view has always been that corporate culture is simply the firm's way of doing business. Is it more than that? Why so much emphasis on it?

"Also, I want to ask about the whole process of ethical decision making. I understand the need for knowledge in making decisions—as well as strong personal integrity and a sense of loyalty to the firm—but when it comes right down to a decision, is there anything beyond these things that I can use to assure myself that I'm doing the right thing? Is there a kind of personal ethics checklist, so to speak?"

DeFario notes, "The contrast between Yoshi and my former employer is nothing short of astounding. The top managers of my previous firm thought of ethics and ethics training as a distraction from the business of earning a profit. There were no clear objectives and no agreement on appropriate behavior other than whatever added to the bottom line. Training was virtually nonexistent. Management left employees to their own devices when it came to making ethical decisions. Senior managers even excused unethical behavior by saying it was really in the organization's best interest. In fact, in order to succeed there, we often had to compromise our ethics. Success was measured in only one way—dollars. Everyone was happy as long as the firm's desired growth and profitability were achieved.

"As a result, most of the people, even those with fairly strong ethical foundations, did their jobs using the "when-in-Rome" rationalization. Talk about living on the high wire! Well, it finally got to be too much for me—and that's why I left."

Glynn comments, "My previous employment situation was not nearly so bad, but much of our so-called ethics program was no more than window

This case was written by Douglas R. Hughes, CFA.

dressing. For example, we had a code of ethics, but it was viewed as a public relations device for external audiences and for legal purposes, not as a guide for employee behavior. It was filled with generalities that gave little or no guidance. The ethics program was, in truth, largely irrelevant to the firm."

> ***Respond to the questions and comments made by the new employees to Wilson.***

Case Discussion

Jeb Wilson has an opportunity with these three employees to explain the elements of corporate culture, including the role of a code of ethics; discuss personal decision making; and contrast Yoshi's attitude toward ethics to those attitudes described by these employees.

Corporate Culture. Wilson could point out that culture has several important functions—to provide a sense of identity and cohesion to employees, to promote commitment by employees, and to provide a basis and direction for behavior. The culture of a firm, whether ethically based or not, influences employees because it affects all aspects of organizational life—from how decisions are made to who gets promoted, how people are compensated, the hours they work, and even what people wear.

The ethical climate of an organization is a critical component of corporate culture; it represents a common understanding of what is correct behavior and how ethical problems will be resolved. This climate is the basis for decision making at all levels and in all circumstances. A climate that supports ethical behavior does not simply happen. Management must give ethical concerns a constant, thorough, and pervasive emphasis if a sense of ethics is to permeate the firm.

Codes of Ethics. Not only does Anthony Glynn raise some common criticisms of many codes of ethics, he also recognizes that a code is often the most visible sign of a company's commitment to ethical behavior—and thus, an essential element in incorporating proper ethical behavior in the corporate culture. A code of ethics cannot, however, address all the areas or situations in which investment professionals practice—particularly if the code is stated in general terms. Moreover, a code is not a sufficient mechanism for ensuring compliance with standards of conduct.

Much of the effectiveness of a code of ethics depends on the nature of the code itself. In order for a code to be meaningful and effective, it must play a central role in the management of ethical behavior within the firm. To play this role, it must have the following characteristics:

▪ *Be specific.* The code's basic principles and expectations must be clearly and specifically stated. It must set boundaries for proper behavior; codes that convey only general principles for conduct are usually not able to provide practical guidance for dealing with specific ethical dilemmas an employee might face. The more explicit the expected behavior, the more likely it is to occur.

▪ *Be relevant.* The code should focus on the potential ethical dilemmas employees could realistically face.

▪ *Be accompanied by training and ongoing communication.* Copies of the code should be distributed to new employees as part of their orientation, and seminars should be regularly conducted on the code for all employees. Each employee should annually sign an affidavit of understanding and compliance with the code.

▪ *Be enforced.* The firm should establish rules for the evaluation of employees' actions in light of the code. The code functions as a deterrent to unethical behavior when it is linked to sanctions for unethical behavior. Procedures to enforce the code, like the code itself, must be descriptive and specific.

Personal Decision Making. During a normal workday, investment practitioners must make countless decisions of various types. Many decisions are not ethically contentious, but many do have an ethical dimension. Jane Sondheim introduces the issue of how she should respond when faced with an ethical dilemma and is trying to decide on a course of action. The critical question is, of course: "Is this action ethical?" An investment professional's ability to analyze an issue from an ethics perspective needs to be nurtured, however, just as investment skills are nurtured.

Sondheim is looking for an "ethics decision-making checklist." Each individual must decide on a personal approach, but ethical training can foster the following useful steps:

- First, determine if a situation does, in fact, have an ethical dimension.
- Second, get all the facts possible.
- Third, list all options.
- Fourth, for each option, ask, "Is it legal, is it right, is it ethical?" For this step, the decision maker may benefit from the assistance of a knowledgeable compliance officer such as Jeb Wilson.
- Fifth, ask, "What are the perceived consequences of my decision for me, my coworkers, my firm, and my clients?"
- And finally, make a decision and take action.

Employer Attitudes toward Ethics. In his previous job, Ray DeFario was in a situation in which decisions were based on corporate greed, an inadequate sense of ethics, improper corporate pressures (the emphasis on the bottom line), and opportunities to engage in unethical practices without fear of firm-induced reprisals. DeFario did the right thing by resigning. One should not have to compromise one's personal ethics to be successful in one's firm.

Glynn described a slightly different corporate attitude, one in which ethics was used simply as window dressing. Nothing is wrong with a firm's ethics program having an external component so long as the communications about the program are carried out honestly and public relations is not the primary reason for the program. Indeed, the message of a strong ethical culture should be communicated to those outside as well as inside the firm. There is no question that good ethics can enhance a firm's overall image. Wilson can turn Glynn's comments to advantage by establishing for Yoshi an honest, straightforward plan to demonstrate how seriously the firm takes ethics by communicating the firm's ethics position to clients and others outside the firm.

Concluding Comment to the Series

Ethical behavior in an investment firm is a complex, multifaceted issue with significant individual and firmwide dimensions. No compliance program, and certainly no amount of training, is by itself going to alter an employee's fundamental character. That character was established before the employee first walked in the door. If an employee has a proclivity toward unethical behavior, not even the most comprehensive ethical program will change that employee.

The vast majority of employees, however, want to do the right thing. But they don't always know how, and they may not even recognize ethical dilemmas when they exist. The behavior of these employees is likely to be favorably influenced by a comprehensive code, compliance policies, and formal ethics training.

Ethics should be an integral part of the daily life and experience of every investment professional. The firm should provide an ethical framework against which employees will be held accountable. In the end, it will protect the integrity of the person and the firm.

Case Briefs

Misappropriation of Investment Opportunity

The Players

Floyd works as a portfolio manager in the High-Yield Bond Department of Ivy International, Inc., a U.S. registered investment advisor. Floyd manages certain unregistered investment funds for Ivy. Square Parts, Inc., is a public company with securities registered with the U.S. Securities and Exchange Commission (SEC).

The Scenario

In October 1990, in connection with an exchange offering, Square Parts issued units composed of subordinated notes, common stock, and warrants to purchase common stock. The Square warrants offered holders the option of paying the exercise price through the surrender of Square notes that, if so used, would be valued at par. The Square notes, although registered, were never listed on any exchange, and from the time they were issued until their expiration in 1994, there was never an active market for them. In July 1992 and again in February 1993, Floyd bought Square notes from Windfall, Inc., a registered broker/dealer, for the investment funds he managed. In January 1993, Floyd learned of the Square warrants while performing research for the investment funds. Shortly afterward, he bought 40,000 Square warrants from Windfall for $11,000 for his personal account. In February, Floyd sold the warrants to another registered broker/dealer for $200,000.

If Floyd had purchased the Square warrants for the investment funds, they would have enhanced the value of the Square notes in the funds' portfolios because the Square notes were trading below par in January and could have been valued at par in exercising the Square warrants. Moreover, the funds were not prohibited from purchasing or holding warrants and were financially able to purchase the Square warrants in January.

Ivy's compliance procedures required that employees preclear any purchase or sale of securities in their personal accounts with the firm's Compliance Department and report personal securities transactions quarterly to the Compliance Department. Floyd failed to seek preclearance and failed subsequently to report his transactions. Because Floyd failed to report these transactions to Ivy's Compliance Department, no disinterested person at Ivy was in a position to determine whether the investment funds, or any of Ivy's other clients, should have acquired the Square warrants.

The Standards

Floyd was not a member of AIMR, but his actions violated at least two of AIMR's Standards of Professional Conduct as well as provisions of the U.S. Investment Advisers Act of 1940 (Advisers Act) and the Securities Exchange Act of 1934 (Exchange Act).

Floyd's undisclosed purchase of the Square warrants was a breach of his fiduciary duty to the investment funds he managed and violated Standard IV(B.1), Fiduciary Duties. The opportunity to purchase the warrants presented Floyd with a conflict between his personal financial interest and the financial interests of the funds. If portfolio managers learn of an investment opportunity of limited availability that is appropriate for certain clients and in which those clients are able to invest, the managers breach their fiduciary duty to the clients if they invest in that opportunity for their personal accounts without disclosing that opportunity to their clients. As a fiduciary, Floyd owed his clients a duty of loyalty that, among other things, required him to offer his clients investment opportunities before taking action himself. As stated in the *Standards of Practice Handbook*, the interests of clients, then of the employer, must take priority over the personal investing interests of the individual manager.

Floyd also violated Ivy's internal compliance procedures, which required that he preclear and report personal securities transactions. By not reporting his personal transactions, Floyd violated AIMR Standard I, Fundamental Responsibilities, which requires that members have knowledge of and comply with all laws, rules, and regulations governing their professional conduct, including any rules and policies set by their employer.

In addition, his actions caused his firm to violate Section 204 of the Advisers Act and Rule 204-2(a)(12) thereunder, which require registered investment advisors to keep and maintain accurate and current records concerning securities transactions by employees with investment discretion.

The Sanctions

As a result of an investigation by the SEC, the investment manager was barred from association with any broker, dealer, municipal securities dealer, investment advisor, or investment company. The SEC also issued a permanent cease and desist order against the manager from further violations of U.S. securities laws governing the manager's conduct.

The SEC's actions illustrate the seriousness with which the SEC views personal trading violations by investment managers. Had the manager been a member of AIMR, the manager would also have been subject to disciplinary proceedings of AIMR's Professional Conduct Program.

Fraudulent Allocation of Trades

The Players

Martin is first vice president and portfolio manager for Halifax, Inc., a registered investment advisor and registered broker/dealer. Martin reports to Pivonka, president of Halifax.

The Scenario

Last year, Halifax served as the investment advisor and principal underwriter for Lynam Investment Fund, a public mutual fund. The fund's prospectus allowed Halifax to trade financial futures for the fund for the limited purpose of hedging against market risks. Pivonka, extremely impressed with Martin's performance in the past two years, directed her to act as portfolio manager for the fund.

For the benefit of its employees, Halifax also organized the Halifax Employee Profit-Sharing Plan (HEPSP). Pivonka assigned Martin to manage 20 percent of the assets of HEPSP, in which Martin participates. Martin's investment objective for the portion of HEPSP's assets that she managed was aggressive growth.

Unbeknownst to Pivonka, Martin frequently placed purchase and sale orders of S&P 500 Index futures contracts for the fund and for the HEPSP without providing the futures commission merchants (FCMs) who took the orders with any prior or simultaneous designation of the account for which the trade was being placed. Frequently, neither Martin nor anyone else at Halifax completed an internal trade ticket to record the time an order was placed or the specific account for which the order was intended. FCMs often designated a specific account only after the trade, when Martin provided such designation.

Halifax had no written operating procedures or compliance manual concerning its futures trading, nor did the firm's Compliance Department review such trading. Martin, after observing the market's movement, assigned to HEPSP the S&P 500 futures contract positions with more favorable execution prices and assigned to the fund the positions with less favorable execution prices.

The Standards

Martin's actions constituted numerous violations of AIMR's Standards. Martin violated Standard IV(B.1), Fiduciary Duties, by failing to place her fiduciary obligation to her clients above her own interests. She favored the HEPSP account, from which, as a plan participant, she personally benefited when the plan's investments performed well.

Martin also should have disclosed her personal interest in the HEPSP account to clients in accord with Standard IV(B.7), Disclosure of Conflicts to Clients and Prospects.

Even if Martin had no personal interest in the investments of HEPSP, her conduct violated Standard IV(B.3), Fair Dealing, by favoring the profit-sharing plan over the fund. Martin owes a duty of loyalty to the participants of the profit-sharing plan, but she cannot show one client favoritism over another.

In addition, Martin knowingly and intentionally caused her firm to violate various record-keeping provisions of the securities laws by failing to designate the time an order was placed or the specific account for which the order was intended. This conduct violated Standard I, Fundamental Responsibilities.

Pivonka, having placed Martin in her position, failed to adequately supervise her by failing to establish appropriate record-keeping and reporting procedures designed to prevent or detect Martin's violations. Pivonka thus violated Standard III(E), Responsibilities of Supervisors. His lack of supervision, including his failure to review Halifax's compliance procedures related to futures trading, caused the firm to violate several provisions of the U.S. securities laws.

The Sanctions
The SEC found that the firm failed to reasonably supervise the portfolio manager with a view to preventing the manager's violations of U.S. securities laws. The SEC censured the firm and ordered that the firm permanently cease and desist from committing or causing any future violations of the Investment Company Act of 1940 and the Advisers Act. The SEC also ordered that the firm pay $9.2 million to be distributed for the benefit of the fund's shareholders, pay a penalty of $300,000 to the Commodity Futures Trading Commission, and retain an outside consultant to implement recommended changes to the firm's compliance procedures. The portfolio manager was barred from association with any broker, dealer, investment advisor, investment company, or municipal securities dealer.

Misrepresentation of Services

The Players
Pierce is branch manager of the Tampa, Florida, office of Daylight Securities Corporation, a U.S. registered broker/dealer and registered investment advisor. Pierce has been working at Daylight for the past eight years. He is a registered representative and advisory representative of Daylight. Pierce recently sat for the Level III Chartered Financial Analyst exam, but he has not received his exam results. He reports directly to Hernandez, Daylight's president.

The Scenario

Recently, Hernandez announced his intention to retire at the end of the year and stated that he would be looking for an energetic, productive, and creative manager to assume his responsibilities. Pierce was thrilled by the announcement, which he saw as an opportunity to prove to Hernandez that he is the best candidate to take over as president. Pierce believes he passed the Level III exam he took in June and expects to receive his CFA designation in the fall. He decides to work extra hard in the next few months to solicit new clients for Daylight to impress his boss.

Pierce plans to hold a financial seminar for Tampa area residents to attract new clients to Daylight. During the next three weeks, he places several advertisements about the upcoming seminar in the local paper. His advertisements contain a picture of a middle-aged man (actually, a picture of one of Pierce's cousins taken from a family photo album) urging readers to attend the seminar and claiming to have attended prior Daylight seminars. A signed quote appears under the picture stating that the Daylight seminar changed the man's life by allowing him to realize his financial goals. The ad also contains a box enclosing a large bold-face caption reading, "Successful Money Management Seminars," with four-point type below reading "financial planning accessible to everyone, presented by Patrick Pierce, CFA III, Advisory Representative, Daylight Securities Corporation, Registered Investment Advisor."

Pierce's advertisements pay off, and attendance for the seminar far exceeds his expectations. As a result, he brings several new clients to Daylight and receives exemplary comments from Hernandez. Thrilled with his success, he places advertisements in several other papers for future Daylight seminars.

The Standards

As a candidate enrolled in the CFA Program, Pierce is required to abide by AIMR's Code of Ethics and Standards of Professional Conduct. His actions, however, constitute several violations of the Standards as well as U.S. securities laws.

First, by placing the advertisements in the Tampa area newspapers, he has violated Section 206(4) of the Advisers Act and Rule 206(4)-1(a)(1) thereunder, which prohibits investment advisors from publishing, circulating, or distributing testimonials of any kind concerning the registered investment advisor or concerning any advice, analysis, report, or other service rendered by such investment advisor. By violating the Advisers Act, Pierce has also violated the Code and Standard I, Fundamental Responsibilities.

Pierce has also violated Standard II(A), Use of Professional Designation, by listing himself in the ad as having earned the "CFA III" designation. There is no professional designation for those individuals who have completed Levels I, II, or III of the CFA exam but not yet received the designation. Pierce hopes to receive his CFA charter in the fall, but he does not know whether he passed the exam or has met all the other eligibility requirements to obtain the designation. Candidates may refer to their participation in the CFA Program, but the reference must clearly state that the individual is a candidate for the CFA designation; the reference cannot imply that the candidate has achieved a partial designation of any type.

Pierce has also violated Standard II(B), Professional Misconduct, by engaging in conduct involving deceit and misrepresentation. He has violated the Code by failing to conduct himself with integrity and dignity and by failing to act in an ethical manner in his dealings with prospective clients and the public at large.

The Sanctions
As a result of the SEC's investigation into this matter, Pierce was censured, ordered to cease and desist from committing or causing any future violation of Section 206(4) of the Advisers Act and Rule 206(4)-1(a)(1) thereunder, and ordered to pay a $5,000 administrative penalty.

Misrepresentations

The Players
Greenberg was an analyst for Blackwater, Inc. She covered a specific industry in which Skyline Industries was a major company.

The Scenario
In November 1990, Skyline's independent outside auditors expressed serious concerns about Skyline's operations. The auditors told Skyline that they would issue a "going concern" opinion of the company—meaning that they believed there was substantial doubt about the company's existence beyond one year without the infusion of additional capital or serious operational changes. Greenberg was aware of the problems Skyline was having and was aware that the auditors would issue a going-concern opinion.

In mid-December, Skyline issued press releases correctly stating the company's situation. Shortly after the releases were issued, Greenberg's husband was hired by Skyline. His compensation included salary of $75,000 a year and a stock option.

The next day, Greenberg drafted a press release for Skyline stating that the previous releases were "incorrect and unauthorized by management and the Board." The new release, in a positive review of Skyline's finances, also stated that Skyline had "increased profits" when, actually, Skyline would probably sustain a loss and noted that "analysts" had made very favorable projections of income, cash flow, and revenue for Skyline.

When asked by shareholders of the company if the projections could be justified, Greenberg replied that "we" had performed due diligence, implying that she and Blackwater had performed extensive due-diligence-type investigations. Greenberg also stated that Blackwater and other analysts who followed the company were the "analysts" quoted in the press release. The company issued the press release written by Greenberg.

The Standards

Greenberg's actions constituted violations of the Code and Standards as well as violations of U.S. securities law. First, Greenberg violated Standard IV(B.2), Portfolio Investment Recommendations and Actions, which requires a member to conduct a diligent and thorough examination when making investment recommendations to others, to have a reasonable and adequate basis for such recommendations, and to make reasonable and diligent efforts to avoid any material misrepresentations. Standard IV(B.2) also requires analysts to use reasonable judgment as to the inclusion of relevant factors in research reports and to distinguish between facts and opinions in research reports. Despite her knowledge of the company's major financial problems, Greenberg made positive statements about Skyline for apparently personal reasons.

In violation Standard III(C), Disclosure of Conflicts to Employer, Greenberg did not disclose to her employer the conflicts of interest that she had concerning Skyline. Greenberg failed to maintain her independence and objectivity as required by Standard IV(A.3).

By drafting a materially false and misleading press release for Skyline, Greenberg violated Standard II(B), Professional Misconduct, which prohibits a member from committing an act that materially reflects adversely on the member's honesty, trustworthiness, or fitness as an investment professional.

Greenberg also violated Standard I, Fundamental Responsibilities, which requires that members have knowledge of and comply with all laws and regulations that govern their professional conduct.

Finally, Greenberg violated the mandates of the Code of Ethics that members must act with integrity, competence, dignity, and in an ethical manner when dealing with the public, clients, prospects, employers, employees, and fellow members.

The Sanctions

Greenberg was found guilty of committing securities fraud [violating Section 10(b) of the Exchange Act, 15 U.S.C. §78j(b) (1988) and Rule 10b-5 thereunder, 17 C.F.R. §240.10b-5 (1994)] by drafting a materially false and misleading press release for a corporation.

The administrative law judge who presided over the case found that

Greenberg not only prepared the untruthful press release but also lied when she asserted that due diligence had been performed that supported her false statements in the press release and held her employer out as sponsoring her views. The judge stated that, whereas a third party, such as an analyst, generally has no legal duty to a company's shareholders, an analyst is obligated to speak truthfully if he or she makes a statement regarding a material fact and permits the company to use it. As a result, the judge held that Greenberg violated a "duty to refrain from making material misstatements in the press release." The judge found that Greenberg knowingly made false and misleading statements in the press release and that the statements were material because they "could have been viewed by the reasonable investor as having significantly altered the total mix of information made available."

The judge also found that Greenberg had violated a duty to Skyline's shareholders. Although Greenberg could not issue a release for Skyline alone, that fact did not absolve her of responsibility, because "analysts play an important role in providing the investing public with an accurate and complete basis upon which to make investment decisions" and public policy concerns should not allow analysts to "avoid responsibility when they permit a company to use their expertise to disseminate misstatements to investors."

Greenberg was barred from association with any broker, dealer, municipal securities dealer, investment advisor, or investment company for three years.

This case serves both to caution the analyst not to become entangled in the preparation or distribution of a press release by a corporation and to remind the analyst of his or her obligation to speak truthfully when making a statement regarding a material fact about a company.

Responsibilities of Supervisors

The Players

Waverly served as the compliance officer and a registered representative for Highland Associates, a registered broker/dealer. He supervised the activities of all registered agents in Highland Associates' local office, including Jameal, Kiddles, and O'Bryan. As compliance officer, Waverly was responsible for oversight of all registered representatives' activities in the Sioux City office and for enforcing Highland's compliance procedures.

The Scenario

While Waverly was compliance officer, Jameal, Kiddles, and O'Bryan committed numerous acts in willful violation of the securities laws. Jameal stole from several clients' accounts by forging customers' signatures on account signature cards and forging checks drawn on clients' accounts; he carried out unauthorized selling of shares in client accounts and submitted false address changes for customer accounts to conceal his conduct. When he was caught, Jameal pled guilty to criminal charges and served a 15-month prison term. Kiddles stole from clients' accounts by forging customer signatures on brokerage documents and on checks drawn on clients' accounts. Kiddles pled guilty to criminal charges and served an 18-month prison term. Finally, O'Bryan was indicted on 13 counts of wire fraud after misappropriating client funds through unauthorized liquidations and by "churning" clients' accounts to receive improper commissions.

The Standards
Waverly's failure to adequately supervise Jameal, Kiddles, and O'Bryan constituted a violation of the Standards and of U.S. securities laws.

Waverly violated Standard III(E), Responsibilities of Supervisors, which requires that all supervisors exercise reasonable supervision over subordinate employees subject to their control to prevent any violations of applicable laws, regulations, or the Code and Standards. Supervisors who are AIMR members, CFA charterholders, and candidates for the CFA designation have a duty to take reasonable measures to prevent such violations. Supervisors must exercise their supervisory responsibility with all employees under their control even if those employees are not AIMR members, CFA charterholders, or CFA candidates. Supervisors may exercise this duty by ensuring that existing compliance procedures are followed and by implementing adequate compliance procedures if none are in place or if existing procedures are not sufficient to detect and prevent violations. Supervisors must make every reasonable effort to detect fraudulent practices.

The Sanctions
The SEC found that Waverly failed to reasonably supervise the registered representatives by failing to enforce compliance procedures and by failing to monitor the activity in customer accounts. He was barred from association with any broker, dealer, investment advisor, investment company, or municipal securities dealer for two years.

Reasonable Recommendations

The Players
Chan, a registered principal and manager of a broker/dealer firm, was retained by O'Hara to manage her brokerage account. O'Hara was a senior citizen with a net worth of more than $200,000 and annual income of more than $41,000. In addition, O'Hara had about $50,000 in cash outside the brokerage account. O'Hara, a widow, had no children and wanted to leave her estate to charity.

The Scenario

At the beginning of the account relationship, O'Hara signed a new-account form that reflected her net worth and annual income. She also wrote that she did not depend on income from her investments for her living expenses. O'Hara's written investment objectives were "income" and "intermediate- and long-term price appreciation."

O'Hara and Chan met about twice a month to discuss O'Hara's portfolio. O'Hara's portfolio consisted of mainly government debt and some corporate debt securities. Initially, O'Hara actively managed her account. She often made independent investment decisions and sometimes relied on Chan's advice. When O'Hara's health began to decline, however, she became less active in her affairs and Chan began to take a more active role in managing her account.

Chan recommended that O'Hara invest in several companies that had experienced operating losses and had little or no expectation of paying dividends. The prospectuses for some of the companies described the securities as highly risky, and some expressly warned that the securities were suitable only for those who could afford to lose their entire investment. In addition, Chan's firm had served as underwriter for some of the companies. Chan maintained that O'Hara had orally agreed to invest 25 percent of her portfolio in each of four strategies: income, income with growth, growth, and speculation. Although some of the investments made a profit, O'Hara suffered losses on others.

The Standards

AIMR members are under a strict obligation to consider carefully the suitability of a particular investment for their clients. AIMR members must ensure that the clients are always fully aware of the policies, strategies, and selection procedures used to invest their funds. Standard IV(B.2), Portfolio Investment Recommendations and Actions, requires members to make a careful effort to determine a client's needs and objectives and to continually review and update the needs and objectives to ensure suitability of the portfolio's investments or strategies.

Standard IV(A.1), Reasonable Basis and Representations, requires members to exercise diligence in making an investment recommendation or taking investment action for others, to support recommendations or actions through research, to maintain supporting documentation, and to conscientiously avoid making any material misrepresentations.

In addition, Standard IV(B.7), Disclosure of Conflicts to Clients and Prospects, requires that members disclose to customers any material conflict of interest that could reasonably be expected to impair the member's ability to render objective advice. In this case, the fact that Chan's firm had underwritten some of the securities he recommended could be construed to impair his objectivity and should have been disclosed to O'Hara.

The Sanctions

The SEC found that Chan's recommendations as a whole were unsuitable for O'Hara's account and upheld sanctions imposed by the National Association of Securities Dealers (NASD). These sanctions included a public censure, a fine of $5,000, a five-day suspension, and a requirement that Chan take an examination to requalify as a registered principal and cease to function as a manager until requalification.

Although the NASD found that Chan acted in good faith, the SEC was "particularly troubled" by the change in O'Hara's portfolio from primarily debt securities to equity securities with substantial risk. The SEC noted that some of the companies had high debt or were thinly capitalized. The commission stated that, although O'Hara did not currently depend on the investments for living expenses, she could need the funds in the future. Even if O'Hara understood Chan's recommendations and decided to follow them, the SEC noted that Chan still had an obligation to make reasonable recommendations.

The Internet

The Players

Van Hagan is a registered investment advisor and broker/dealer trying to find new ways to reach customers and expand her existing business. She is also principal and sole employee of Greenlight Investments.

The Scenario

As a cost-effective method of advertising, Van Hagan created an Internet home page on the World Wide Web. On the page, she extolled her firm's performance, stating that "returns using the AIMR Method exceed 20 percent!" In addition, she posted a "free research report" as an example of what clients would receive if they subscribed to her research service.

Although Van Hagan's calculations and composites were made in accordance with AIMR's Performance Presentation Standards (PPS), she did not make the disclosures mandated by the PPS, such as the use and extent of leverage and whether results were calculated gross or net of management fees.

The research report Van Hagan posted on the Internet was one she had prepared a year previously for a high-net-worth individual recommending purchase of a small-capitalization stock. Van Hagan posted only part of the research report because it was a "freebie," and she deleted some of the report's detailed financial information on the company's past business and its stock's expected rate of return.

The Standards

Van Hagan's actions violated several provisions of the Code and Standards. First, Standard V(B), Performance Presentation, states that members shall not make any statements that misrepresent their investment performance. Second, because Van Hagan's presentation did not make the required disclosures, she cannot claim compliance with the PPS. Although compliance with the PPS is voluntary, once a member claims compliance, the presentation must be in compliance with *all* the requirements of the AIMR PPS. Also, use of terms such as "AIMR method" or "AIMR-compliant" is in violation of the PPS.

Standard IV(A.1), Reasonable Basis and Representations, requires that members and candidates make reasonable and diligent efforts to avoid any material misrepresentation in a research report or investment recommendation. Because the report was a year old, the passage of time may have made some of the information in the report materially misleading.

Also, under Standard IV(B.2), Portfolio Investment Recommendations and Actions, Van Hagan has a responsibility when making an investment recommendation to ensure that it is suitable for the client. Because the Internet reaches such a broad range of individuals, not solely the high-net-worth individuals targeted in the report, Van Hagan may not have met her obligation of suitability.

In addition, Standard IV(A.2), Research Reports, states that members and candidates must indicate the basic characteristics of an investment when preparing for general public distribution a report that contains an investment recommendation. Basic characteristics include, among other things, current and expected rate of return, degree of marketability/liquidity, and business, financial, and market risk. By deleting some of this crucial information, Van Hagan did not fully represent the true nature of the investment and its characteristics when posting the report. That the original report contained this information is irrelevant; what was presented to the public via the Internet was deficient.

The Sanctions

Under the Code and Standards, members are required to maintain knowledge of and compliance with all applicable laws, rules, and regulations governing their conduct. Failure to maintain required knowledge and compliance constitutes a violation of Standard I, Fundamental Responsibilities. This brief is purely illustrative, but provisions of the Advisers Act, other U.S. securities laws, and state laws could have applied to Van Hagan's activities. Moreover, Van Hagan's activities could have been subject to rules of the NASD or other self-regulatory organizations.

Conflicts and Disclosures

The Players
Robertson, a CFA charterholder, worked for Big Firm, a registered broker/dealer and investment advisor, as a senior broker in the Pension Division. Robertson was well known within the industry as an expert in pension investments, and he knew many people in the field. Investments Inc. is a registered investment advisor and broker/dealer trying to sell its investment products and services to the pension market. Ivan, a CFA charterholder, is an advisor with Investments Inc.

The Scenario
Robertson agreed to provide Investments Inc. with advice about the pension market, introduce Investments Inc. to pension fund boards, and recommend Investments Inc.'s products and services to pension fund boards. In return, Investments Inc. agreed to pay Robertson a monthly consulting fee and a finder's fee for referring purchasers. The arrangement began while Robertson was employed by Big Firm and continued after Robertson left Big Firm and started his own company, New Firm, which he controlled.

Robertson did not inform his clients of the referral and compensation arrangement with Investments Inc. Investments Inc. did not inform others, through any of its written materials or otherwise, of its arrangement with Robertson because it believed it had an exemption from certain legal requirements mandating disclosure. Several companies, including Valley Company, hired Investments Inc. on Robertson's recommendation without knowledge of the relationship.

The Standards
Ivan's belief that he was not under a legal obligation to disclose Investments Inc.'s payment of referral fees to Robertson was erroneous. Even if he had no legal obligation to disclose, however, Ivan was under a duty to adhere to the requirements of the Code and Standards, which mandate disclosure.

Ivan violated Standard IV(B.8), Disclosure of Referral Fees, which directs all members, candidates, and CFA charterholders to inform clients and prospective clients of any consideration paid or other benefit delivered to others for recommending the member's services to that prospective client or customer. Consideration includes all fees, whether paid in cash, in soft dollars, or in kind. Ivan should have informed Valley Company of the. arrangement before entering into any formal agreement for services with the company. Ivan should also have disclosed the nature of the referral arrangement; for example, whether payment was made as a flat fee or percentage, one time or continuing, based on performance or providing research (or other noncash benefit), and the estimated dollar value of the payment. Valley Company needs this information to fully evaluate the impartiality of Ivan's recommendations of any services and the full cost of the services rendered.

Robertson violated Standard IV(B.7), Disclosure of Conflicts to Clients and Prospects, which requires members, candidates, and CFA charterholders to disclose any material conflict of interest that could reasonably be expected to impair the member's ability to render unbiased and objective advice. Robertson's clients should have had all relevant data needed to evaluate the objectivity of Robertson's recommendation. Information about the relationship between Robertson and Investments Inc. would help clients determine whether Robertson's advice is truly objective.

Robertson also violated Standard III(D), Disclosure of Additional Compensation Arrangements. Under Standard III(D), Robertson should have informed Big Firm in writing of the nature of his compensation from Investments Inc. for recommending their products and should have updated the disclosure as necessary. Employees have a duty of loyalty to their employer, and multiple employer relationships can create a conflict of interest between responsibilities to competing employers. Big Firm should have had full information regarding Robertson's competing interests so that it could evaluate the effect of those interests on Robertson's ability to serve Big Firm effectively.

The Sanctions

The SEC ordered the firm to pay $500,000 and cease and desist from any further violations of the disclosure and antifraud provisions of the Advisers Act and the Exchange Act. The broker was permanently barred from association with any broker, dealer, investment company, investment advisor, or municipal securities dealer, and the registration of the broker's new firm as an investment advisor was revoked.